Freshly Brewed Volume Two

Seven one-act plays from Bewley's Café Theatre

Freshly Brewed Volume Two

Seven one-act plays from Bewley's Café Theatre

Selected for publication by David Horan and Stewart Roche

Edited by Declan Meade and Sara O'Rourke

The Stinging Fly

A Stinging Fly Press Book

2 4 6 8 10 9 7 5 3 1

Published in association with Bewley's Café Theatre
in November 2019.

Copyright © individual authors, 2019.

Set in Palatino
Printed by Walsh Colour Print, County Kerry

The Stinging Fly Press
PO Box 6016
Dublin 1
www.stingingfly.org

ISBN: 978-1-906539-80-1

The Stinging Fly gratefully acknowledges funding support from
The Arts Council/ An Chomhairle Ealaíon.

Contents

Introduction by David Horan vii

John Sheehy *Fred & Alice* 2

Billie Traynor *The Importance of Being Honest* 34

Malachy McKenna *The Quiet Land* 60

Katie McCann *Cirque des Rêves* 94

Ciara Elizabeth Smyth *All honey* 138

Caitríona Daly *Normal* 198

Stewart Roche *Wringer* 224

Introduction

Bewley's Café Theatre is proud to be a home for new writing in Irish theatre. The boutique nature of our venue and its lunchtime format might insist that we present only one-act plays with certain limitations when it comes to larger production elements. However, the Café Theatre—and indeed the nature of theatre itself—never imposes limits on the imagination of playwrights. Proof is here in the variety of style, form and subject matter contained in this collection.

We promote new writing by either commissioning work from established theatre artists or by providing a platform for the best of what is presented elsewhere throughout the island of Ireland. Together, the seven plays in this collection represent work by emerging writers, established playwrights and senior Irish theatre artists. All have successfully created brilliant roles for actors, intriguing stories for audiences and complete worlds for directors and designers to explore, imagine and re-imagine. We hope this collection encourages new productions at home and abroad so that audiences beyond the Bewley's stage can delight in them anew.

Fred & Alice by John Sheehy is a quirky love story about two people who find each other in a care facility and together they take on the world. They are the narrators of their own story, so they create this world together as well, with giddy abandon. It all makes for an anarchic and unsentimental comedy that manages to remain childlike and utterly unique.

Cecily Cardew and Gwendolen Fairfax, the female leads of Oscar Wilde's *The Importance of Being Earnest,* are resuscitated in Billie Traynor's sequel. It's twenty years after the pair were married to the Ernests of their dreams and both are still as different as chalk and cheese. The suffragette movement is in full swing and, along with an ancient Merriman, the women are forced to look afresh at their place in the world. Apart from being hilarious and an admirable homage to Wilde, full of epigrammatic wit, *The Importance of Being Honest* manages to also draw interesting parallels between Gwendolen and Cecily's world of 1913 and our own.

The Quiet Land is Malachy McKenna's celebration of the humour, resilience and endearing innocence of an older generation as it struggles to survive in the rural Ireland of today. Originally performed by two great actors of the Irish Theatre, Des Keogh and Derry Power, the conversation may be of a gentler time. But there's nothing gentle about today's conversation. They are forced to confront each other with some heart-breaking truths.

Katie McCann's *Cirque Des Rêves* is a ghostly tale with Dickensian overtones theatrically told by four versatile actors who portray more than twenty characters—mostly tawdry ones—along with performing original music and song. Following the adventures of Poppy Parker, an ordinary girl who encounters a remarkable circus and uncovers a dark power waiting to be set free. It's pure theatre.

All honey by Ciara Elizabeth Smyth is a laugh-out-loud farce for the twenty-first century. Ru and Luke are throwing a house-warming party. They intend to warm their house. But their guests seem more interested in whispering in the box room than joining the festivities. Explosive characters and unfolding secrets mean there's more to clean up than red wine stains and glitter in this five-character twenty-something comedy that becomes an arch satire on the nature of contemporary romance.

Caitriona Daly's beguiling play, *Normal,* brings to light the needs of someone living with autism. Beautifully crafted, it's a post-birthday-party showdown between the mother and the new girlfriend of Gary, who is on the spectrum. A tug-of-war ensues. A tug-of-love. Daly has created two superior roles for women, and ultimately her play becomes an arresting portrait of love in difficult circumstances.

Finally, Stewart Roche's *Wringer* is a three-hander thriller that grips tight. When fading movie star and raconteur Jonathan Ravenciffe agrees to an interview with up and coming blogger Elsa, he anticipates an evening of anecdotes about his time with Hammer Horror, working with Roger Corman and acting in cult TV shows from the 1980s. What he hasn't bargained for is Elsa's ability to dig deep into his past. A past that may or may not contain a very dark secret. When the cameras stop rolling, the horror begins. And with it, a very modern story with #MeToo associations unfolds.

I would like to thank all the playwrights for allowing us to publish their work and Stewart Roche, particularly, who led on this project. I'd especially like to thank Iseult Golden and Colm Maher for their work as Producer/Administrator of the Café Theatre and Technical & Front of House Manager. They are a vital part of the work that Bewley's does. They are the spirit of the venue. I'd also like to thank the founders of our theatre, Kelly Campbell and the indefatigable Michael James Ford, who along with the rest of our board members tirelessly support the work each and every day.

It takes a community to run a theatre and we'd like to acknowledge here the great talent, dedication and hard work of so many theatre artists who have graced our little stage over the years.

Bewley's Café Theatre is proud to acknowledge the continued support of the Arts Council and Dublin City Council. We look forward to publishing a third volume of *Freshly Brewed* plays, hopefully in the not-too-distant future.

David Horan
Artistic Director
Bewley's Café Theatre

Freshly Brewed Volume Two

Fred & Alice

John Sheehy

With the support of Ballyhoura Development, Fred & Alice *previewed in Friars' Gate Theatre, Kilmallock, County Limerick, on 23rd March 2012. It subsequently played at Bewley's Café Theatre in February 2013.*

DIRECTOR: John Sheehy
PRODUCER: Cora Fenton for Callback theatre
DESIGNER: Olan Wrynn
LIGHTING DESIGNER: Tim Feehily
SOUND: Cormac Brennock
COSTUME DESIGNER: Joan Hickson
MARKETING DESIGNER: Jason Cook
VIDEOGRAPHY: Jeff Manning

CHARACTERS & CAST:

FRED: Ciarán Bermingham
ALICE: Cora Fenton

John Sheehy works extensively as a writer and director and is co-founder of CallBack theatre. His other plays to date include *Set in Stone, Men Without Souls, The Hole, Dog Shit City* and *Janey Dillis*. He has adapted some of his plays for radio, winning a PPI National Radio bronze medal for drama with *Fred & Alice*. John has previously been awarded Theatre Artist in Residence for two years in Friars' Gate Theatre by The Arts Council. Upcoming projects include an adaptation of *Janey Dillis* for radio and a script for a new comedy to premiere next year. John also works as a director and Project Manager for CallBack's touring plays including *Fred & Alice*, which has had over 160 performances to date nationwide.

Present Day.

A Wendy house type structure Up Stage Centre. One box Stage Right that can be used to sit on and store the following props: ALICE's squash racket, a bucket with water, a picture frame. Two boxes Stage Left that can be used to sit on and also store the following props: FRED'S tennis racket, earphones, FRED and ALICE finger puppets, the MOTHER wooden spoon puppet and a cardboard cutout of a car. A standing lamp is tucked away Stage Left.

ALICE: (*Offstage*) Go go go…

Enter FRED.

FRED: You play guitar by pressing your fingers down on the strings. By doing this you change the strings' length, causing them to vibrate and make different sounds. Shortening a string makes it sound higher and lengthening it makes it sound lower. Different strings produce different sounds depending on how thick they are.

Of course sound is just energy made by vibrations. When a string vibrates, it disturbs the air particles around it. These disturbed particles bump into the particles close to them, which makes them vibrate too causing them to bump into more air particles until they are all disturbed. This movement keeps going until they run out of energy. If you are close enough to all this disturbance you hear the sound.

When vibrations hit our eardrums a message is sent to the brain and it interprets it as sound. Nobody knows how or why the brain decides its music though. There are many different types of music.

Acappella… Aak… Aaroubi… Abaimajani… Abajeños… Aboriginal rock… Abstract hip hop… Abwe… Acoustic Techno Fusion… Acid croft... Acid house... Acid groove... Acid jazz... Acid punk... Acid rap... Acid rock... Acid techno... Adai-adai... Aduk-aduk... Adult contemporary... Anti-Serious Music... African blues... African jazz... Afrobeat...

ALICE: (*Offstage*) Fred...

FRED: Afro-Cuban jazz... Afro-Cuban rumba... Afro-juju... Afro-Kaiya... Afro... Afro-punk... Afro-soul... Afro-zouk... Afroma

ALICE: (*Offstage*) Fred...

FRED: Aggrotech... Aguinaldo... Ahouach... Ahidus...Air... Akyn... Alb-pop... Aleatoric music... Algerias... Alomaco... Alpine New Wave... Alpunk... Alternative country... Alternative... Alternative metal... Alternative punk...

ALICE: (*Offstage*) Fred, you're boring people.

FRED: No, I'm not.

ALICE: (*Offstage*) Yes, you are.

FRED: But I'm talking about music.

ALICE: (*Offstage*) That's the problem.

FRED: Everybody likes music.

ALICE: (*Offstage*) Yes, but not as much as you.

FRED: What should I say then?

ALICE: (*Offstage*) Begin at the beginning.

FRED: In the beginning... in the beginning... I had better start before the beginning.

ALICE: (*Offstage*) Oh sweetest Jesus.

FRED: Before the beginning. I have been told that there was a time when neither I nor Alice existed. This seems unlikely. But then one foggy Christmas Eve a great light appeared in the eastern sky and people all over the world knew that something monumentous was going to happen and then a great flash of lightning ripped the sky in two and then…

SOUND: ALICE Intro Music. Enter ALICE

ALICE: I was born. I'm pretty sure that's not the way it happened because my birthday is in June. But I like Fred's way of telling it. I don't know much about when I was born except that it was a sad time. My father died during childbirth. My mother never talks about it. All she ever said about him was that he was a dramatic man that upstaged her every chance he got. I don't know, I don't remember. Fred remembers being born, don't you Fred? (*FRED shudders.*) And by the time he was one year old, Fred had completley mastered the English language. But Fred's really modest so he didn't tell anyone. Freds was so modest he didn't say anything for a few years. They thought he was dumb.

FRED: Dumbass.

ALICE: Hee hee. Dumbass. They didn't think he could talk until he was seven or eight, in the convent. It wasn't really a convent but there were a lot of nuns.

FRED: Lot of nuns.

ALICE: Lot of nuns. Fred grew up in the convent because he didn't have parents, only a father and his father was disappointed at Fred when he was small.

FRED: Dumbass.

ALICE: So he left. So Fred lived in the convent and when he was seven or eight he started talking and he was saying all these words that nobody had taught him and he was saying sentences that they couldn't even understand so they got scared and called the doctor and Fred was taken away, away from his playmates and the people he had known all his life, the closest thing he had in this world to family.

FRED: I didn't mind.

ALICE: Fred didn't mind. And then they put him in a home. It wasn't really a home but Fred always called it a home because that was where he lived, and if you are not living at home then where are you?

FRED: Where the hearth is.

ALICE: Home sweet home.

FRED: Home on the range.

ALICE: There's no place like home.

FRED: Home Alone.

ALICE: Home and Away.

FRED: Home to roost.

FRED: Sweet Home Alabama.

ALICE: It's my turn Fred… I can't think of any more.

FRED: Alice's mother says she knew from the look of her that there was something wrong with Alice. Even when Alice was a small baby she looked sad and bewildered, her mother said.

ALICE: There's nothing wrong with being sad and bewildered. It's a perfectly natural reaction to an ever changing world.

FRED: She said it wasn't natural for a baby to never laugh. There was something amiss she said.

ALICE: But Fred says he remembers what it's like to be a baby and it's a very stressful and depressing time.

FRED: Alice's mother is a right bitch.

ALICE: A right bitch. She's very nice though. She looks after me.

FRED: You can look after your self.

ALICE: No, I can't.

FRED: I'll look after you.

ALICE: Will you, Fred?

FRED: I will. Alice didn't go to school. Her mother kept her home and minded her. Alice was very friendly but she had no one to make friends with. Poor Alice.

ALICE: Poor Alice.

FRED: Mother taught Alice to read and write, taught her right from wrong. Taught her Holy God loves her and that she would probably go to hell. Poor Alice.

ALICE: Poor Alice.

FRED: Mother's friends came to visit. They said she was a great woman.

ALICE: So patient.

FRED: A saint. Mother says she was only doing her duty and not to take any notice of Alice. Sorry about Alice. Alice is on the Whirly-gig. Poor Alice.

ALICE: Poor Alice. Alice says she is moving out.

FRED: Mother says no.

ALICE: Alice says she is going anyway.

FRED: Mother says, remember the kitten. Remember the kitten, Alice.

ALICE: Poor Alice.

FRED: (*Beat.*) Watch this.

ALICE: What?

FRED: You.

ALICE: Oh yeah.

FRED: Look before you leap.

ALICE: 17

FRED: Our lives are like a candle in the wind.

ALICE: 31

FRED: God, if I can't have what I want, let me want what I have.

ALICE: 41

FRED: And in the end, it's not the years in your life that count. It's the life in your years.

ALICE: 65

FRED: Life is like a hot bath. It feels good while you're in it, but the longer you stay in, the more wrinkled you get.

ALICE: 85

FRED: And so on.

ALICE: 7

FRED: We are finished now, Alice.

ALICE: 21

FRED: The game is over.

ALICE: 13

FRED: It's not funny any more.

ALICE: 18

FRED: It was never funny.

ALICE: 15

FRED: It's just annoying now.

ALICE: 18

FRED: Alice

ALICE: 5

FRED: Stop

ALICE: 4

FRED: Now

ALICE: 3

FRED: Or

ALICE: 2

FRED: 1

ALICE: 1 (*FRED laughs victoriously.*)

ALICE: Right.

FRED: Said Fred.

ALICE: Right.

FRED: Said Fred.

ALICE: Right.

FRED: Said Fred.

ALICE: Right.

FRED: Said Fred.

ALICE: Right.

FRED: Said Fred.

ALICE: Right.

FRED: Said Fred. (*ALICE is getting nervous*)

ALICE: Right.

FRED: Said Fred.

ALICE: Right.

FRED Said Fred.

ALICE: Right.

FRED: Said Fred.

ALICE: We can't go on like this forever.

FRED: Said Fred.

ALICE: Please stop it, Fred.

FRED: Said Fred.

ALICE: Please stop it.

FRED: Said Fred.

ALICE: Please stop.

FRED: Said Fred.

ALICE: Please.

FRED: Said Fred.

ALICE: Fred.

FRED: Said Fred.

ALICE: Fred.

FRED: Said Fred.

ALICE: Right.

FRED: Said Fred.

ALICE: Right.

FRED: Said Fred.

ALICE: Right.

FRED: Said Fred.

ALICE: Right.

FRED: Said Fred.

ALICE: Fred.

FRED: Said Fred.

ALICE: I don't want to do this any more.

FRED: Said Fred.

ALICE: Right.

FRED: Said Fred.

ALICE: Right.

FRED: Said Fred. (*This continues for some time.*)

ALICE: Maybe we should have the interval now.

FRED: There is no interval.

ALICE: Said Fred. (*ALICE laughs victoriously. ALICE mouths the word 'Right' before continuing.*)

ALICE: Fred loves music. It's his whole life, Fred could just sit in his room and listen to music the whole time.

SOUND: *Rock music*

FRED: Someone's banging on the door.

ALICE: Someone's banging on the door. Fred.

FRED: Someone's banging on the door.

ALICE: What's all that noise?

FRED: What's all that noise.

ALICE: It's three o'clock in the morning.

FRED: Put your headphones on.

ALICE: Put your headphones on, Fred.

FRED: I'm putting them on. (*FRED puts his headphones on, music stops.*)

ALICE: Fred tried to tell his music teacher that music was subjective. The music teacher told Fred that he hadn't a note in his head. Fred says that all the notes are in his head and that might be the problem. If Fred had his way he would talk about nothing but music. But they taught him that if he wanted to get along he would have to talk about other things and take an interest in other things. For a long time Fred decided that he didn't want to get along, but he came around, didn't you, Fred? (*No answer.*) Well most of the time anyway. Remember how we met, Fred? Do you want to tell it? I'll tell it. We met in the home.

The one I went to when I was on the whirly-gig or when my mother needed a break from me. We were lucky that we ever met because on the day I started they were threatening to throw Fred out of the home because of the incident. They only let him stay because he had been there so long and he had no place else to go. Fred was an institution within an institution. I don't mean to be mysterious but we never talk about the incident.

FRED: I burned the kitchen down.

ALICE: Fred burned the kitchen down.

FRED: I told them it was an accident.

ALICE: You weren't allowed in the kitchen.

FRED: They told me to take an interest in other things.

ALICE: But not at three o'clock in the morning.

FRED: I'm a great cook.

ALICE: You're a terrible cook, Fred. And you burned the kitchen down.

FRED: Plenty of people burn their kitchens down.

ALICE: Yes, but they don't laugh when it happens.

FRED: I burnt the dinner.

ALICE: Okay, but you shouldn't have told them you were a terrorist.

FRED: I never said that.

ALICE: Yes you did. You said it was an act of culinary terrorism.

FRED: Culinary terrorism.

ALICE: Fred loves words but he doesn't show off. When he learns a new word he wraps it up and stores it away. Then sometimes if you ask him or if you are stuck, Fred will bring it out and unwrap it and say it for you.

FRED: Discombobulation.

ALICE: But most of the time he is happy just to know where it is stored.

FRED: Supurflous.

ALICE: Fred says that without words we would have nothing to talk about. (*Pause.*) Which is probably true when you think about it. He also says that without words we wouldn't even be able to think.

FRED: Cererbral.

ALICE: I'm not so sure about that.

FRED: Chronological.

ALICE: Fred loves words but they don't love him.

FRED: Asparagus.

ALICE: Now picture this…

FRED: Sarcophagus.

ALICE: Hang on, an example is worth a thousand pictures. What's this word, Fred? U-R-I-N-E

FRED: Urine.

ALICE: Is it though?

FRED: Urine.

ALICE: Maybe its Uriiine.

FRED: Uriiine? Urine. (*Mouths the words then builds up a mantra.*) Urine uriiine urine uriiine. (*Underscores*)

ALICE: Sometimes if he finds a word he likes or if he thinks of two different ways of saying a word he gets stuck. I thought it was really funny the first time I saw him do it. Then one night I tried it, just for fun. Beep. I said beep over and over again and after a couple of minutes I thought I was going to lose my mind so I stopped. I've seen Fred do it for hours. It scares me. (*Shouts*) It's all piss, Fred. (*FRED stops. Beat.*) He's still doing it in his head. When he does the word thing it's mostly in his head. He was only doing it out loud for our benefit, weren't you, Fred? (*No answer.*) He could answer if he wanted to but he is being belligerent.

FRED: I'm still doing it in my head. It's okay. It's like having a radio on in the background. Sort of. It will work away and run its course. When I'm finished with urine uriiine I might have to do Beep for a while. Thanks, Alice. Once I start with a word I won't stop until it's finished. It's like having a job to do and I'm employee of the month. No, that's not right. It's more like I have to keep doing it until I get it right. Until it's right.

I love words. And that confused them. I love music, you see. And I love words. They said I should only love one thing so I could fit neatly into one of their boxes. Well, a pox on their box.

ALICE: A pox on their box. A pox on their box. A pox on their box. A pox on their box.

FRED: Don't… don't get me started. What they couldn't understand is that I do only love one thing. What they couldn't understand is, words are music, and sometimes the record is scratched or there's a digital glitch. It's usually okay. I haven't had a bad one for a long time. They told me it wouldn't kill me, even the bad ones. Which is true, I think.

They told me I wouldn't lose my mind either. Sometimes when I'm stuck, I can feel it slipping away. It starts off with me repeating and repeating. Once I have built it into a mantra my control begins to slip and it becomes its own thing. We are co-existing now and it's a delicate thing, like a bubble. And I think I could make a big effort, even at this stage and stop. Burst the bubble. But I don't want to. Then the mantra begins to take over and I begin to recede. Now I can feel the hairs on the back of my neck begin to stand up and it's getting cold. It's in the room with me now. I can feel the power of its presence and it's scary but it's exciting as well. I can hear the mantra but it doesn't feel like it's coming from me any more. It's its own thing now and I can't stop it. From the corner of my eyes I see the world begin to blur. The mantra goes on and I feel like I'm on the long drag to the top of the world's tallest rollercoaster.

ALICE: *(Beat.)* Anyway, when I was eighteen I started going to the home where Fred lived. I was sitting in the middle of the corridor crying my eyes out because I had spilt a glass of milk all over myself. I now realise that, that was a disproportionate reaction to a minor accident but at the time I was in crisis. Then Fred came walking down the hall and it was the first time he spoke to me and I'll never forget it, he stood looking down at me and he said, and I'll never forget what he said. He said…

FRED: Get up.

ALICE: Get up, he said.

FRED: Get up.

ALICE: So I did. And that was that, love at first sight. Well, for me anyway. Fred didn't talk to me again for years. That was okay because I cope with rejection really well. Then eventually Fred got used to me and it was love at first sight for him too.

FRED and ALICE touch fingers shyly for the first time. On the touch SOUND: Ballerina Music. ALICE spins like a dancer in a music box. They become aware of what they are doing and stop. Music stops.

ALICE: I always want to be friends with everybody but not everybody wants to be friends with me. Fred's got the opposite problem. He doesn't want to be friends with anybody.

FRED: That's not true.

ALICE: That's not true. Fred's got a whole community of music friends that he talks to on the internet. But he doesn't like any of them.

FRED: That's true.

ALICE: That's true. Fred was unusual and not just for obvious reasons. He stayed at the home all the time. Not like me or most people. I just came in the morning and went home in the evening. The only times I stayed were when I was having one of my turns or when my mother needed a break from me. The only ones that stayed in the home were the quiet ones that slept or stared most of the time. Fred wasn't like them. I asked the nurse why Fred was there when he wasn't like the others and she said that Fred had spent so long in care that now he was institutionalised and there was no place else for him to go. They had tried training Fred in a load of jobs but he wouldn't do them. Fred doesn't work well with others.

FRED: Or by myself.

ALICE: Or by himself. I used to see Fred everyday. We sat in a circle and talked with the doctor in the mornings, Fred was there but he never said anything. I used to talk a lot. About anything really until they said it was time to give someone else a go. I asked if I could have Fred's time as well but they said I couldn't. Which was very unfair I thought. Fred wouldn't have minded. He told me so when he started to talk again. Fred had stopped talking. When it was lunchtime he ate in silence, when it was fine and some of us went out to play basketball he watched in silence and when we watched tv he watched in silence. He was like the opposite of me. This was during the years before we were going out, before Fred knew I was alive. Though he told me afterwards that he knew alright.

The thing about Fred was that he refused to accept his diagnosis. They tried to tell him what was wrong with him but he wouldn't listen. Maybe he is delusional because Fred says there is nothing wrong with him. Fred says give a dog a bad name and he'll bark all night and he isn't going to bark for anyone. Fred says that he's Fred and I'm Alice and anyone that says we are anything else can go fuck themselves.

FRED: Go fuck yourselves.

ALICE: Go fuck yourselves. I shouldn't use language like that. Fred says I should use any any language I feel like using. I love Fred. So all this time I'm watching Fred and he hasn't said a word to anyone for years and I notice that he has a tennis racket that he carries everywhere with him, except he doesn't carry it around like a normal person or even like a... person. He's got it on a strap and he carries it on his back. Now this strikes me as being a bit odd because Fred doesn't play any sports. And we don't have a tennis court. We have table tennis (*Beat.*) but that wouldn't work. One time I pretended to have one of my turns so that I could stay in the home for a couple of days and I peeked in to

Fred's room and he was sitting on the bed with his earphones on and he had the music turned up really loud because I could tinny hear it from the doorway and he was playing along on the tennis racket like it was a guitar and it was… it was beautiful. That's what Fred did every single night in his room. As soon as I could I got a racket of my own and I went along to Fred's room and I sat on the chair opposite and I started to play as well. And Fred sat watching me for a long time and then out of the blue he started talking again. He said…

FRED: You're doing it wrong.

ALICE: And then he took off his headphones and gave me half, so I could hear the music properly. It was really romantic. Then he started to show me how to play properly and from then on we practiced every spare moment. (*FRED teaches ALICE how to play the racket as a guitar.*) Fred may have had all the notes in his head and not be able to play a single one but that wasn't going to stop him having a music career. After that me and Fred were really close. Sometimes we even finish each other's…

FRED: Sandwiches.

ALICE: Hee hee, sandwiches.

FRED: Unless they're ham.

ALICE: Fred doesn't like ham.

FRED: Fuckin pigs.

ALICE: Pig in a poke.

FRED: Pig in a blankct.

ALICE: Pig on a spit.

FRED: Pigs in shit.

ALICE: Pigs will fly.

FRED: Pigs in space.

FRED: Piggy in the middle.

ALICE: Damnit... The doctors were delighted that Fred was talking again and they said it was all thanks to me. They said I was good for Fred, that I brought him out of himself. But he was good for me as well. He pushed me back into myself a bit. I mean, sometimes when we are playing I almost stop thinking. Soon I realised that it wasn't a tennis racket that Fred played, it was...

FRED: A James Trussart Deluxe Steelcaster, rated the third coolest guitar in the world by musicradar dot com.

ALICE: Rated number one by Fred. Three weeks later we played Wembley... The concert is a sell out and the stadium is heaving and Fred has a chair wedged under the door handle in case we are interrupted. I've never seen such a crowd and I'm not sure I can go out there. Fred is coping better than me.

FRED: Hello, Wembley. I love words. I love music. I love you, Wembley.

ALICE: And Wembley loves Fred and 90,000 people scream his name.

FRED: Fred, Fred.

ALICE: My stomach is churning and I'm burping butterflies. Fred warned me about stagefright. He says the body can think it is under threat and have a fight or flight response.

FRED: Fight or flight. Here's a little song for everybody out there.

ALICE: And I desperately want to either run for the hills or beat someone to death with my guitar.

FRED: Live fast and die young. All we need is love.

ALICE: Blood pressure is elevated as my body primes itself for action. Heat builds up in my vital organs and my face turns bright red.

FRED: Fight or flight. Flight or fight.

ALICE: Muscles contract throughout my body and begin to tremble. My vocal cords are stretched and my voice tightens.

FRED: We love you, Wembley.

ALICE: And now Wembley is screaming my name as well.

FRED: Alice Alice Alice Alice

ALICE: Fred

FRED: Alice

ALICE: Fred

FRED: Alice

ALICE: Fred

FRED: Alice

BOTH: Fred Alice (*Repeat…*)

FRED: Someone's banging on the door.

ALICE: Someone's banging on the door?

FRED: Someone's banging on the door.

ALICE: Who's that banging on the door, Fred?

FRED: Your mother's banging on the door.

ALICE: Why's my mother banging on the door, Fred?

FRED: Your mother is a bitch and she's banging on the door.

ALICE: My mother is a bitch and she's banging on the door.

FRED: Your mother is a bitch and she's banging on the door.

ALICE: She wants to know what we were doing with the door locked, but it's kind of hard to explain.

FRED: So we don't say anything.

ALICE: Mother decided God was wrong and now I'm on the pill.

FRED: No mistakes now, Alice.

ALICE: No mistakes.

FRED: Remember the kitten, Alice.

ALICE: Remember the kitten.

ALICE: It's just a matter of keeping count of them and I'm good at that.

FRED: Except for the time you took them all at once.

ALICE: Except for the time I took them all at once. I wanted to see what would happen.

FRED: What happened?

ALICE: I had morning sickness.

FRED: And afternoon sickness.

ALICE: And evening sickness.

FRED: And night-time sickness.

ALICE: I took them properly after that. Fred was invited to my house for dinner.

FRED: No thanks.

ALICE: He had to come anyway and he was on his best behaviour. Fred did not say one word the whole time he was there. (*Beat.*) Blah, Blah, Blah, Blah, Blah, Blah, Blah, Blah, Blah, Blah, Blah…

FRED: Alice's mother talks a lot.

ALICE: She does. (*Beat.*) My mother asked Fred if he was institutionalised. He thought about it for a long time, then when he got back to the home went upstairs and packed everything he owned into one suitcase. Then he came downstairs and took me by the hand. We walked out the door, down the path and out through the gates. I don't think Fred ever went that far on his own before. We walked down the street until we came to a crossroads. Then Fred stopped. We stood there for a long time, holding hands. Watching the traffic go past. Watching it get darker and darker. (*SOUND: Cars passing.*) But you didn't give up, did you? Fred marched back to the home and announced to everyone –

FRED: We're moving in together.

ALICE: They said we couldn't but then after a while they said we could. If my mother agreed.

FRED: Alice's mother had to sign a lot of forms but she had to read them first. Alice's mother is a really slow reader.

ALICE: I read them faster than her and they said.

FRED: They said…

ALICE: They said that we could get our own home and live a life of complete and utter freedom. (*Beat.*) With the following provisions. Number 1: Someone from the home would visit once a month, to say hello and talk about the weather.

FRED: Objection.

ALICE: Overruled. (*Beat.*) Number 2: We had to have this button that when you push it, it starts ringing loads of people.

FRED: Objection.

ALICE: Overruled. (*Beat.*) Number 3: My mother comes to visit twice a week and stays as long as she wants.

FRED: Objection.

ALICE: Overruled. (*Beat.*) Number 4: Fred had to do a training course to learn how to make wicker baskets.

FRED: Objection. Objection. Objection.

ALICE: Overruled. Overruled. Overruled. (*FRED gets into a huff.*) Who's going to make the wicker baskets, Fred? They wouldn't ask you to do it if it wasn't important. All those bits of wicker lying around the place. Someone has to make baskets out of them. It turned out that Fred was very good at making wicker baskets.

FRED: There is no such thing as wicker. We made baskets out of willow. They should be called willow baskets. Most people are bad at making them but it's easy. There are many different types of wicker basket. Asian fishing basket, the Boston bread basket, the Cantonese weaving basket, the Danish…

ALICE: You don't have to explain, Fred. Just show them the picture. (*FRED shows picture of basket.*) Fred brought home the very first wicker basket that he made. We keep it on the mantlepiece.

FRED: Alice's mother finished reading the forms but she hasn't signed them yet. Alice's mother is a really slow writer.

ALICE: I write faster than her.

FRED: You never write.

ALICE: Yes I do.

FRED: What do you write?

ALICE: I wrote you a Christmas card last year.

FRED: Dear Fred. Happy Xmas. Alice.

ALICE: And I wrote you a Valentine's card.

FRED: Dear Fred. Happy Valentine's. Alice.

ALICE: I'm working on your Birthday card.

FRED: My birthday is months away.

ALICE: Waiting 1,2,3.

Waiting 1, 2, 3, 4. Happy Birthday, Fred.

Waiting 1, 2, 3, 4, 5. Another Christmas.

Waiting 1,2,3,4,5,6,7. Another Valentine's.

Waiting 1, 2, 3, 4, 5, 6, 7, 8, 9, 10, 11, 12, 13, 14, 15...

I'm always counting. I like it. They told me that it was an immature coping strategy but I think that an immature coping strategy is better than no coping strategy. Anyway it's more than just a coping strategy. I really like counting. I love it.

1, 2, 3, 4, 5, 6, 7, 8, 9, 10, 11, 12, 13, 14, 15, 16, 17, 18, 19, 20, 21 and on to the forever.

I used to think if you could count fast enough or in the right way you could catch it out.

I like three's. It's amazing that no matter what the number, it could be close to the start or close to forever but it will always be only one or two away from being divisible by three. I am perfectly aware that every number is at most only one away from being divisible by two but two is a boring number. Three is more… friendly. It's more… right.

And if you count in three's you get there three times as fast.

3,6,9,12,15,18,21 and so on to forever.

Better still you could leave out the three's altogether.

1, 2, 4, 5, 6, 7, 8, 9, 10, 11, 12, 14, 15, 16, 17, 18, 19, 20, 21, 22, 24, 25, 26, 27, 28, 29, 40

It may not seem faster at first but you have to think big. Imagine counting to 4 trilliion.

2,999,999,999,999,999,995… 2,999,999,999,999,999,996… 2,999,999,999,999,999,997… 2,999,999,999,999,999,998… 2,999,999,999,999,999,999…

4 trillion.

Even better again if you leave out all three's and multiples of three

1, 2, 4, 5, 7, 8, 10, 11, 14, 16, 17, 19, 20, 22, 25, 26, 28, 29, 40

The fun really starts if you take the numbers you are left with, divide them into groups of three, like (1,2,4) is one group (5,7,8) is the next one, then (10,11,14) and so on. Then all you have to do is add the single digits within each group and if the total adds up to a three or a multiple of three then you have to leave out all the numbers in that group.

So it's like 1+2+4= 7 and that's okay…

5+7+8= 20 and that's okay…

10+11+14 is 1+0+1+1+1+4 is fine because they add up to 8.

16+17+19 is 1+6+1+7+1+9 = 25 – thumbs up!

20+22+25 is 2+0+2+2+2+5 =13…

Ooops. That won't do! So we have to leave those numbers out.

So now we are left with:

1, 2, 4, 5, 7, 8, 10, 11, 14, 16, 17, 19, 26, 28, 29, 40

FRED: Alice has been on the Whirly-gig for a while now. No that's wrong. Alice has been in wonderland for a while now. She is extra happy and is excited about everything but wonderland only lasts for so long... (*FRED and ALICE touch fingers and the distorted ballerina music plays. It stops when FRED sits ALICE down Stage Right.*) then it's time for Alice 20,000 leagues under the sea. She says it's like being in a glass coffin 20,000 leagues under the sea. She can see out but all the pressure of that water keeps her pinned down. She says that one day the glass will crack and shatter and that will be the end of Alice.

ALICE: (*Distant.*) I had the dream again...

FRED: (*Realises she is not going to continue.*) Alice had the dream again. It's like having a near death experience. Alice is up high, looking out through a small window, like an aeroplane window. (*FRED frames ALICE's head with the window frame.*) She is looking down on herself lying on a bed. I'm there and Alice's mother is there as well. Alice's mother is wearing the dress with the red flowers that she always wears when she has to go somewhere she doesn't want to. And there are doctors there as well, the ones from the telly that are usually really funny but now they are all acting really serious. Alice is looking down on all this from her little window that is too small for her to fit through. Out of the corner of her left eye she can see blackness that goes on for ever and ever. She wants to call out to us but when she opens her mouth no sound comes out. Out of the corner of her right eye she can see blackness and blackness. Now she's getting scared and she has a feeling that there is something behind her. Down in the room we are all being really quiet. The feeling that there is something behind her gets too much and Alice glances back over her shoulder but all there is, is blackness. When she looks back the window is gone and all there is, is blackness and blackness, forever and ever. We better go.

ALICE: I just want to sit here for a while.

FRED: We should go now.

ALICE: I just want to sit here.

FRED: Okay.

ALICE: You'll look after me, Fred, won't you? (*Beat.*) I remember the kitten. "The scraggy wee shit. His soft paws scraping like mad." I never wanted a kitten. I never asked for a kitten. My mother said she was trying to teach me responsibility. Fred says she was trying to teach me the opposite. That I could never be responsible. I don't know. I love my mother. I love Fred. I never wanted a kitten. I was only young then. Younger anyway. And I never asked for a kitten. I got home one day and there it was in a box looking out at me. My mother said it was mine and I had to look after it. It had evil eyes and scratchy nails and I didn't want to go near it. She said I had to feed it but I said I wouldn't. She said she wasn't going to either and the poor thing was going to starve to death if I didn't feed it. My mother had bought the kitten food and said all I had to do was open the bag and pour it in the bowl. But I couldn't do it. I never asked for a kitten.

After a couple of days it was crying constantly. It had learned to climb out of the box and it followed me around when ever it saw me. And it never stopped crying. Mewling and mewling and mewling and… And it was cruel to let the thing starve to death. So one day I filled a bucket full of water and I threw it in. It splashed around for a bit then it climbed back out and flopped on to the ground. I didn't know they could swim. It's not mewling anymore now. It's just standing there shivering, tiny with its hair glossed flat. I can't stop now so I get a board and a big rock. I pick the kitten up and it's all wet and sticky and I throw it back in the bucket. Then I slam the board on top and weigh it down with the rock. It's only a little thing but I can hear it banging against the side of the bucket and scratching at the board. And it goes on forever. After a while I go back inside and sit down and wait. Watching the clock. I wait a full hour and then I go back outside. The board is still on top of the bucket, weighed down by the rock and it's quiet. It's really still and it's too quiet and I can't go near it. So I go back inside and act weird for the rest of the night. My mother found it the next day. She made me look at it before she buried it. Then she said I could get into big trouble but it was okay. She wouldn't tell anyone. I finally confessed to Fred.

FRED: It was only a bloody kitten.

ALICE: Then he showed me a poem about drowning kittens.

FRED: "Isn't it better for him now, glossy and dead."

ALICE: The poem made me feel sad but it made me feel better as well.

FRED: Alice wants to look at everything at once. If she could she would cover the whole world with floodlights. But you can't see anything that way. You have to focus. (*FRED gets FRED puppet, sets up boxes Stage Left and uses Stand Up lamp to light puppet playing area.*) You need a tight spotlight on one thing and then if you are lucky, you might see something. Just focus on one detail and then nothing else matters. (*FRED uses FRED puppet.*) Alice? Are you there?

ALICE: (*ALICE uses ALICE puppet.*) I'm here. I don't like this.

FRED: Focus.

ALICE: I don't like this. We are too small.

FRED: We are not small enough. If we were smaller we could see what the table is made of.

ALICE: The table is made of wood.

FRED: If we were smaller we could see what the wood is made of.

ALICE: Wood is made of wood.

FRED: No. It's made of little tiny atoms.

ALICE: What holds them all together?

FRED: We do, because we believe that they are all held together to make a table.

ALICE: I believe in tables.

FRED: I believe in tables too. (*They clap 3 times*). And we could see all the tiny particles of air floating above the table.

ALICE: Can I count them?

FRED: No there are too many.

ALICE: How many?

FRED: I don't know.

ALICE: I should count them.

FRED: Focus. If we were smaller still there would be only one particle of air.

ALICE: Just one?

FRED: Fred and Alice on one particle of air.

ALICE: Just one?

FRED: Just one.

ALICE: I think I like that.

Enter MOTHER puppet.

MOTHER: What do you think you are playing at? This isn't a game. Do you hear me? Answer me dammit. I hate you Fred, do you know that?

FRED: I don't mind.

MOTHER: You can't take her away.

FRED: You can't keep her.

MOTHER: She is all I have.

FRED: She is all I have.

MOTHER: She needs looking after.

FRED: She can look after herself.

MOTHER: No she can't.

FRED: I can look after her.

MOTHER: Can you Fred?

FRED: Yes.

MOTHER: And who will look after you?

FRED: Who will look after you?

MOTHER: Who will look after me.

FRED: You can come visit us.

MOTHER: I will.

FRED: On Tuesdays and Saturdays.

MOTHER: I could come and cook dinners.

FRED: On Tuesdays and Saturdays.

MOTHER: I could help…

FRED: On Tuesdays and Saturdays.

MOTHER: Alright Fred. (*Goes to exit*) I'm not a bitch, Fred.

FRED: Okay.

FRED: Alice's mother drove us to our new house. (*Use cardboard cutout of car with the puppets.*)

ALICE: But Fred said she couldn't come in because it was a Wednesday (*Exit MOTHER*). Bye, Mammy.

FRED: Bye, Mammy.

SOUND: Travelling Music. FRED and ALICE set up the Wendy house.

BOTH: Our House.

FRED and ALICE get in to the house and look out through the windows.

FRED: It started with a pizza box

ALICE: 14-inch thin crust pepperoni

FRED: And two empty Coke cans

ALICE: One diet, one regular

FRED: Then another pizza box

ALICE: 14-inch thin crust pepperoni

FRED: And two more cans of Coke

ALICE: As before

FRED: Then another pizza box

ALICE: 14-inch Meat Feast. Tired of pepperoni already

FRED: By the end of the week the table is full

ALICE: And we are sick of pizza

FRED: What to do?

ALICE: I can cook pasta and sauce

FRED: I push every thing on to the floor to make room

ALICE: Four days later and there isn't a pot left in the house

FRED: And the sink is full

ALICE: What now?

FRED: Chipper

ALICE: Big tasty with bacon

FRED: Double quarter pounder with cheese

ALICE: Large fries and Coke with everything

FRED: Whopper, Angus and a Big King

ALICE: Taco fries, onion rings and nuggets

FRED: Zingers and chicken in buckets

ALICE: Two Cokes with everything

FRED: Closed

ALICE: Found the microwave

FRED: I like the microwave

ALICE: Even Fred can cook in the microwave

FRED: And ready meals

ALICE: So many ready meals

FRED: It's endless

ALICE: Chicken Curry With Rice

FRED: Chicken Jalfrezi With Rice

ALICE: Chicken Korma With Rice

FRED: Chicken Tikka Masala with Rice

ALICE: Chicken Rice Chinese Style

FRED: Beef Hotpot

ALICE: Roast Beef In Gravy

FRED: Beef Lasagne

ALICE: Carbonara Beef

FRED: And Red Wine Casserole

ALICE: Sweet and Sour Chicken

FRED: Sweet Chilli Chicken

ALICE: Chicken Balti

FRED: Chicken Chow Mein

ALICE: Szechuan Chicken and Noodles

FRED: Cottage Pie

ALICE: Cumberland Sausage Pie

FRED: Shepherd's Pie

ALICE: Fisherman's Pie

FRED: Ocean Pie

ALICE: Ocean Crumble

FRED: Tesco Light Choices Chicken

ALICE: And Prawn Paella

BOTH: Crispy Salad, Crispy Salad, Crispy Salad, Crispy Salad…

FRED: So many ready meals.

ALICE: I'll never be hungry again.

FRED: And two litre bottles of Coke.

ALICE: One diet and one regular.

FRED: I can't see the floor any more.

ALICE: And not just because you are getting fat. Sorry.

FRED: Soon it's up to my waist and I have to wade everywhere.

ALICE: My mother came to visit. (*Knock on door.*) Hi, Mammy – but Fred wouldn't let her in.

FRED: Couldn't open the door. Bye, Mammy.

ALICE: We are up to our necks in it now and I'm starting to get nervous.

FRED: We are awash in a swelling sea of empty bottles and cartons

ALICE: Paper and plastic.

FRED: We try to push it back

ALICE: To take back what is ours

FRED: Till it looms over us

ALICE: Growing everyday

FRED: Solid as a landslide

ALICE: Then one night when we were trying to wade to bed

FRED: It came crashing over us like a tidal wave.

ALICE: All of a sudden, I'm under. And it's dark and peaceful but I can't breathe. I start to kick out for the surface and nearby I can hear Fred do the same. I swim up through pizza and anchovies, up and up through shoals of sandwich wrappers. I'm nearly through when I get caught in a rip tide of uneaten crispy salad and I'm dragged under again.

BOTH: Crispy Salad, Crispy Salad, Crispy Salad, Crispy Salad…

ALICE: I manage to fight my way clear and just when I think my lungs are going to explode I break through the surface. (*FRED and ALICE burst through the roof of the Wendy house.*) I tread rubbish and take deep gasping breaths as Fred does the back stroke.

FRED: I like it.

ALICE: It's nice up here but we are too close to the lightbulb and my skin is beginning to blister. We can't live like this, Fred.

FRED: I like it up here.

ALICE: I'm burning up, save me, Fred. Fred takes a deep breath and dives down into the depths. Three times he dives and the last time he comes up he has a triumphant look in his eye.

FRED: I pulled the plug.

ALICE: Then slowly the room begins to spin and the level begins to drop. (*FRED spins the Wendy house.*) Then faster and faster and its turning into a giant whirlpool. Round and round and down and down and I'm afraid we are going to be sucked down the drain. Faster and faster and down and down and then we spill out into the garden.

FRED: (*Beat.*) We tried to keep the place a bit cleaner after that.

ALICE: Then we lived happily ever after, because me and Fred discovered that the way to be happy is to accept your limitations. You accepted their limitations didn't you, Fred?

FRED gives two fingers to audience. ALICE gets the rackets and FRED gets the headphones.

ALICE: We don't need those any more, Fred. No one's going to bang on the door.

FRED: No one's banging on the door?

ALICE: No one's banging on the door.

FRED: No one's banging on the door.

SOUND: Musical Finale finishing with thunderous applause from Wembley crowd.

FRED: Thank you, Wembley.

ALICE: And Goodnight.

THE END

The Importance of Being Honest
by Billie Traynor

First produced at Bewley's Café Theatre in October 2014.

DIRECTOR: **Liam Halligan**
SET DESIGNER: **Eoin Lennon**
COSTUME DESIGNER: **Helen Connolly**
LIGHTING: **Colm Maher**
SOUND: **Eamonn Murphy**

CHARACTERS & CAST:

GWENDOLEN MONCRIEFF: Billie Traynor
CECILY MONCRIEFF: Noelle Brown
MERRIMAN: Eamon Rohan

Billie Traynor is an actress and writer who lives in Dublin. She started to write for theatre in the early 2000s, as advancing years brought to her notice the dearth of decent roles in theatre or film for the older woman. Other plays include *Redser*, *Out of Service*, *Life after Love*, and *Beryl and Eejit*.

An English Manor House garden, high summer. There is a small table and two chairs Downstage Centre with a pruning shears and basket on it, along with several books and pamphlets. There is a large plinth bearing a plant Stage Left. Another small table Upstage Right bears a gramophone.

Cecily Moncrieff enters, carrying a gentleman's silver topped cane and a white rose. She turns and waves to someone Offstage.

CECILY: Goodbye my dearest! Please take great care of yourself! (*She turns to place the flower on the table Stage Centre, smells the bloom, then notices the cane in her other hand. She moves swiftly Downstage Right*) Dearest! Your cane…

She tails off as she watches a car drive down the curving driveway and out through the gates. She smiles wryly then moves to the chair Stage Left and places the cane on it. She removes the wrap she is wearing over a diaphanous Isadora Duncan style dress, then goes to the gramophone Upstage Right and winds up the gramophone to start playing Schubert's Musical Moment No. 3 - piano version. She begins to dance in the style of Isadora Duncan, dancing all around the space. MERRIMAN, an extremely old and decrepit butler, enters and crosses shakily to her. She continues to dance as he speaks.

MERRIMAN: Excuse me, Miss Cecily… er… Mrs Moncrieff… er… I thought I should remind you, ma'am, that it's the second footman's day off, and the butler has gone to visit his dying mother. Most inconvenient! And now another visitor has arrived… a lady… er… (*examines a card on his tray*) no, no, no, this cannot be correct… er… the lady says she is (*squints furiously at the card*) Mrs Moncrieff! Impossible!

CECILY: (*Momentarily puzzled.*) Mrs Mon… (*She stops dancing, beginning to panic.*) Good Heavens! Gwendolen!

MERRIMAN: (*Triumphantly remembering.*) Good Heavens – Gwendolen of course!! Miss Gwendolen… er… the other, er, Mrs Moncrieff, is here to see you… I, er, brought her to the library, but when I turned around she wasn't… I, er… don't quite know where she's got to, Ma'am…

CECILY: (*She frantically grabs the dressing gown from the back of one of the chairs and flings it on.*) Dear dear Gwendolen! This is just her way, to arrive unannounced… No doubt she's doing her usual inspection of my house, simply ensuring that standards are being maintained… she performs the same service for me in town, don't you know? Such an obliging friend. (*Gritted teeth.*) And you say she's wandered off… well, she'll find me when she wants to! Thank you, Merriman… (*He turns to leave.*) Oh, and you may bring tea in a little while. (*She waves him away vaguely, he creakily leaves.*).

MERRIMAN: (*Sotto voce.*) Tea. And the footman gone and the butler… tea… and a woman wandering the grounds! (*Exits Stage Right.*)

CECILY studies the table and chairs, then dusts them vigorously with the hem of her robe. She notices the pamphlets on the table, picks them up along with the books, gasps, and dashes to place them beside the gramophone. She again wipes the chairs, this time dusting the legs as well. She steadies herself, closes her eyes and begins to chant

CECILY: Hmmmmmm… every day, in every way, I am getting better and better. Every day, in every way, I am getting… Oh no! His cane!!

She places it Upstage Right behind the plinth… She wipes back her hair, finds the daisy chain, flings it into her basket, calms herself. Enter GWENDOLEN, who spends a minute or so observing CECILY while taking notes in a small notebook. CECILY notices her and they smile tightly, GWENDOLEN moves to embrace CECILY.

CECILY: Dearest Gwendolen!

GWENDOLEN: My darling little Cecily!

They air kiss and CECILY indicates the chair Stage Right, which GWENDOLEN runs a gloved finger over, checks it, and smiles at CECILY, ignoring the invitation to sit and starting to remove her gloves in an agitated manner.

CECILY: I hope your journey was pleasant?

GWENDOLEN: As pleasant as can be expected, since the public railway system somehow became affordable to every ragtag, bobtail and Irishman in the country. There were no first-class carriages available, but a kindly local Minister offered me a seat in his. I soon became extremely sorry to have accepted, as he surreptitiously drank from a large unmarked bottle for most of the journey, and snored for the rest.

CECILY: Oh, my poor sweet Gwendolen! Had I known you were reduced to… I… would have sent the carriage…

GWENDOLEN: It is of no importance, dearest girl. My darling Ernest had taken the car… some business of parliament, I believe… though I take great care never to involve myself in the minutiae of my husband's life. Knowledge of one's husband has been the downfall of many a happy marriage. My mother's doctrine of sublime ignorance of the ways of men should be adopted by every young girl entering the wedded state. If it is not adhered to, there are many shocking experiences in wait for the innocent bride… I myself have applied Mama's teachings in every way, and voila! Ours, I am glad to say, is the happiest of marriages!

CECILY: Indeed, Gwendolen, indeed! No-one could doubt your devotion to my loving guardian, nor his to you… when he is at home…

GWENDOLEN: (*Stiffly.*) Indeed. Dear dear Ernest's parliamentary duties have become quite… onerous of late. But this, my sweet little girl, is part of the burden of those of us who have some… standing in Society. You and your Ernest, of course, live a very quiet and dull life, of your choice, I am sure, but MY Ernest could never be without the… cut and thrust of the political life. Even though of late he has had to sacrifice a great deal of our time together, he does not shirk his calling. A calling in which, of course, he does much good for those who are less fortunate than ourselves…

CECILY: Ah yes… the ragtag and bobtails who, thanks to his last bill, can now afford to travel by train… ah, here is tea!

MERRIMAN enters Stage Right with a large tray, which he proceeds to shake all the way over the table, staggering back slightly as he starts to place it. He finally succeeds in doing so, but there is tea, milk, sugar etc. spilled on it. He slowly takes out a large cloth and proceeds to try to mop it up.

MERRIMAN: (*Trying hard to remember.*) Tea, yes, and milk and… but there was something… something else… er… (*Suddenly remembering.*) Ah yes! (*To both.*) Cake, or bread and butter?

BOTH: (*Glance at each other, then vehemently.*) Neither! (*GWENDOLEN can stand it no longer.*)

GWENDOLEN: That will do!

CECILY: (*Offended.*) Thank you, Merriman, that's delightful. We ladies can look after ourselves now…

MERRIMAN bows creakily and slowly shuffles back in the direction of the house, muttering.

GWENDOLEN: Really, Cecily, don't you think it time Merriman was… retired?

CECILY: Oh, not Merriman!

GWENDOLEN: There are many young men seeking employment, and I am sure he has given countless years of service…

CECILY: Put poor Merriman out to grass? (*Pouring milk in both cups*) Oh, dear Gwendolen, I simply couldn't! Merriman has looked after me since I was little, and now, in his old age, I feel responsible… (*shocked look from GWENDOLEN.*) and I wouldn't have had him serve tea, except it's the footman's day off… I couldn't bring myself to upset poor dear old Merriman. (*Picking up the sugar bowl, questioning – sugar??*)

GWENDOLEN: (*Waving aside the sugar.*) Sentimental as ever, poor little Cecily! Really, dear, you must soon grow up a little and take over the household reins with a firm hand! I know of nothing that pleases a man so much as a well-run household… in my experience, my household management skills have pleased my Ernest more than my many other attributes… why, he often comments on the efficiency of our arrangements. Only the other day, he compared my boudoir to a hospital ward in its… ah yes, its "clinical functionality". Darling man! (*During this speech, CECILY: has slyly placed three sugar lumps in GWENDOLEN's cup*)

CECILY: How very flattering! I'm afraid MY Ernest has never deemed it necessary to comment on my skills in the boudoir... (*Sharp look from GWENDOLEN.*)

GWENDOLEN: (*Accepting cup.*) Hardly surprising, since you seem to constantly dress as if you were in one!!! You are becoming excessively modern, dear Cecily, for one who was raised with the greatest care by my Ernest!

CECILY: It is surely a woman's duty to become modern... at least as modern as her husband will allow! And my dear Uncle Jack... your Ernest, of course... was the most liberal of guardians. My only conservative influences came from Miss Prism... and we both know the origin of her rigidity only too well...

BOTH: The handbag...

GWENDOLEN: (*Sighs and sips from her cup, a look of satisfaction spreading over her face*). Cecily, I must enquire from your cook as to the origin of your tea! I never enjoy a cup of tea so much as when I visit you!

CECILY: (*Smiling.*) How very sweet!! And I, for my part, always enjoy preparing it for you!

GWENDOLEN: My dearest Cecily! It is so nice to know that at least one person in one's life can be relied upon... will remain true...

She sits reflecting for a moment, then stands and walks towards the plinth where CECILY has disposed of the walking stick. CECILY leaps up and joins GWENDOLEN, trying to shuffle her away.

CECILY: Perhaps you should rest, Gwendolen? Your trying journey on public transport must have fatigued you considerably, and I'd hate to send you back to Uncle Ja-... Ernest I mean – in an exhausted state!

GWENDOLEN: You are most considerate, little Cecily, always thinking of others... As I always say, I knew from the moment we met that we were destined to become friends... thank you, dear, I shall sit, although I feel sufficient... agitation... to prevent me from relaxing in the least...

CECILY: (*Taking her elbow and moving her back to her seat, away from the cane.*) Agitation, Gwendolen? Still? Surely your discomfiture with the inebriated vicar has faded by now?

GWENDOLEN: Oh it is not the vicar who upsets me so, dear... indeed I wish it were! I have dealt with many an inebriated gentleman in my time, and no doubt will have to again... these modern times are so trying to the distaff of the species. We find ourselves contending with a lack of basic courtesy in men which would have appalled our mothers! Modern men think nothing of appearing before a lady in a state of complete undress – why, only last week one of Ernest's colleagues in parliament sat at my dinner table sans bow tie! My butler had to be revived in the kitchen with smelling salts, and the soup was so delayed as to be stone cold when served. When I expressed my dismay to Ernest, he simply smiled and said this sort of thing is becoming more and more acceptable, and a good thing too! I was shocked, dear Cecily, I tell you – shocked! If my Ernest, the very pillar of our social circle, can accept behaviour of this sort – behaviour which I believe is more than common in the Commons, dear – where will it all end? Shall we have opera in morning dress? Dinner in tennis whites? The thought is too horrible to countenance!!

CECILY: (*Sitting her down gently.*) Dear friend! Please try to calm yourself – I have some sal volatile in the house...

GWENDOLEN: (*Sitting.*) I have never indulged in chemical remedies, nor shall I ever, Cecily. The introduction of foreign chemicals to the female system is highly undesirable. Who knows what the end results might be? Women are as highly tuned as racehorses, and must be treated accordingly. I have never allowed my grooms to administer anything to my horses but the most basic and natural of remedies. I myself only use laudanum, and even then only in extremis. Forgive me, Cecily, I shall be quite myself in a moment...

CECILY: (*Sitting.*) Of course

They sit in silence for a moment, GWENDOLEN becoming more agitated, CECILY puzzled. MERRIMAN slowly creaks into view and crosses to CECILY.

MERRIMAN: Shall I, Mrs Moncrieff? (*Glaring balefully at GWENDOLEN* *as she turns to him along with CECILY.*) Miss Cecily? (*Indicating the tea tray.*)

CECILY: Yes, thank you, Merriman… but perhaps you could bring a small carafe of hock… (*Turning to GWENDOLEN.*) I find it very calming, in moments of distress, to sip a cool glass of wine while sitting in the garden…

MERRIMAN: Hock. Hock? Yes. Carafe. Tray. Kitchen. Scullery. Cellar. Tray. Garden.

MERRIMAN bows and staggers off in the wrong direction with the tray, heading Stage Right where the cane is concealed. CECILY rushes to him and physically turns him round, knocking the cane over as she does. She then attempts to kick the cane back into hiding. GWENDOLEN glances at her, then stares at her awkward attitude. CECILY smiles blithely and stretches her arms over her head, swinging her leg energetically.

CECILY: Exercises! Dear Isadora Duncan! Don't you just love the dance, dear Gwendolen? (*Saving herself and sitting demurely once more.*) I do so love to go down to the lake in the mornings and let nature inspire me, waving diaphanous fabrics about me like a… goddess of the mist… my dance teacher studied with Isadora herself, and has endeavoured to impart to me that – spirit – of abandonment. Don't you agree that dance is the most liberating of the arts, Gwendolen?

GWENDOLEN: In its place, dear girl, in its place! Really, Cecily, you will do yourself an injury with this foolishness! Women of our age must remember the demeanour of our dear mamas, and try to emulate it! I myself mourn the age of full corsetry for its wonderful… uprightness and rigidity! I am afraid the current fashion for looseness of dress and… (*delicately*) undergarments is undermining women's attitudes to the world.

CECILY: Ah but this… looseness of dress, which I have to say I find gives great physical ease to women, surely contributes to an ease of mind!

GWENDOLEN: Ease of mind is all very well, so long as it is not applied in everyday life. We need only witness the disgraceful behaviour of those females who believe the vote to be an entitlement!

CECILY: Ah but it surely is, dear Gwendolen… I for one would like to think that our daughters would have the same control over their destiny as every young man does…

GWENDOLEN: Our mothers would be so shocked at the behaviour of these fanatical young women.

CECILY: (*Hastily changing the subject at GWENDOLEN's stare.*) I, of course, never knew my dear mama, I'm afraid. Dear Miss Prism was my only model of motherhood, and she… (*Shakes her head a little.*) I do hope that has not affected my bringing up of my two darlings in any way, Gwendolen?

GWENDOLEN: (*Sweetly.*) Indeed not, dear little Cecily. Your two lambkins are as precious and wonderful as can be – I regard them as being almost as wonderful as my own two darlings. Your Jemima is almost as pretty as my own dear Augusta, and I believe your JohnJohn constantly comes second in class at Oxford to my Cecil! You must be so proud!

CECILY: (*Smiling sweetly.*) Thank you, dearest Gwendolen. Your compliments are always so… perfectly formed!

GWENDOLEN: Complimenting others is an art, my dear Cecily, which should be taught in our public schools. I myself make a point of complimenting others at every available opportunity, especially when they don't deserve it, which sadly is very often…

MERRIMAN: (*Staggering in with the wine and two glasses on a tray.*) Hah! I found it! The hock… it was in the cellar… yes, hock!

CECILY: Ah, lovely! Our remedy for all distress, Gwendolen! (*Pouring a glass of wine for both of them. MERRIMAN exits Stage Right.*)

GWENDOLEN: Distress, my dear girl? Distress? I myself am never distressed, I am happy to say… Or at least not publicly. Public displays of emotion are to be avoided at all cost, at least among the upper orders. The lower echelons of society, of course, display their affections and sorrows for all the world to ignore… (*bitterly*) and what could possibly distress our dear little Cecily, she of the perfect husband, home and servants?

CECILY: Oh, but I am not... (*Distressed... silence.*) I do hope, dear Gwendolen, that your visit to the country will help... will relieve whatever agitation you are feeling...

GWENDOLEN: I believe it will, dear girl, and without the aid (*gently pushing her glass of wine away disdainfully*) of intoxicating liquor, the use of which I have never approved of before 4 o'clock. (*She stands and walks towards the plinth, gazing into the distance, breathing deeply.*) Ah yes, the country! Do you know, dear girl, every time I come here I feel I can – almost – understand how my dear Ernest could miss it! And then of course I return to London and the real world, and forget all about (*breathing in again*) the wonderful clean air and gentle living that my Ernest reminisces about. Gentle living... one does so wonder what he means by that...

CECILY: (*Rushing over Upstage of GWENDOLEN, blocking the cane.*) Er... yes, one does, I suppose... but then this – gentle living, as he calls it – is all I've ever known, dear Gwendolen... and until my lovely Uncle Ja... your Ernest... went to live in London with you, he had lived here for the longest time, you know... ever since he was...

BOTH: Found in a handbag...

GWENDOLEN: I do sometimes wish that I had never known of Ernest's origins... that is, his being – found – although of course his true pedigree is impeccable, and that is all that matters...

CECILY: Indeed. Pedigree. Though not all that matters, I would have thought? In, er, a marriage? Is that... I mean, really... (*GWENDOLEN turning to her, looking puzzled*) all? (*Drinking her wine, not looking at GWENDOLEN.*)

GWENDOLEN. I'm sure I don't know what you mean, dear girl. All? But of course pedigree is everything! To marry beneath oneself would be a great tragedy, don't you realise? Your little life has been so... sheltered, so... protected! You have never witnessed the depredations of the Season, nor I believe even been presented at Court! Such an innocent!

CECILY: (*Through gritted teeth.*) Not so innocent as you might think, dear Gwendolen! At least in the ways of married life...

GWENDOLEN: (*Shocked.*) Cecily! My dear, you go too far!

CECILY: I simply meant...

GWENDOLEN: I do not wish to hear it, Cecily. I have already disclosed to you my view of the modern woman and her place in the world. Do not distress me by disclosing details of your... private... life...

CECILY: I would not dream of doing so, Gwendolen, I only meant that... I believe that in marriage both partners deserve to be equally fulfilled and happy. I believe that women deserve more from life than living to comply with their husbands' views. (*A little nervously.*) Even to the point of... (*in a rush*) women being allowed to vote and stand for Parliament!

GWENDOLEN: You see! You have become infected with modernity, Cecily! What nonsense! With regard to voting, once a woman has chosen the right partner in life, she can relax in the knowledge that he will decide on matters outside the home, on which front she is the sole mistress. Women have the right to maintain domestic control. That is what matters. It is from that domain of direction and power that they send out their men to rule the world in the way in which they have been... guided... by their wives. As to marriage, it is a contract between a man and a woman, within which neither has the right to seek his or her own happiness! Marriage is an arrangement for the betterment of Society and the world, dear girl, and to produce offspring for the perpetuation of the upper classes. That is all.

CECILY: (*Under her breath.*) All indeed! (*To GWENDOLEN*) But what if... one of the parties to a marriage is... dissatisfied with those terms? What then, dear Gwendolen?

GWENDOLEN: Dissatisfied? (*Picking up her glass and knocking it back.*) With a proper marriage? I really do not understand what you can mean, dear Cecily. How can a man be... dissatisfied... with a perfect marriage? (*Bitterly*) With a perfect wife? (*Pouring another glass of wine, knocking it back.*) With a perfectly kept household? How? (*Turning to CECILY, really appealing to her. CECILY is a little taken aback.*)

CECILY: Perhaps dissatisfied is not the correct word... perhaps... tired and longing for... something else... explains it better?

GWENDOLEN: Explains what, exactly, dear Cecily? Are you speaking of your own marriage, perhaps? For I fail to see how this subject of… longing… dissatisfaction… applies to my state at all… (*She stands and walks towards the hedge again, turning back again to walk Stage Centre. CECILY dives over to grab the cane, and shoves it behind her back, goes over to the table, refills both glasses, rings the bell. Gwendolen turns to look at her.*) Are you quite well, my dear? I feel your association with the dance of your Miss Duncan may have done you some injury?

CECILY: Quite well, thank you, Gwendolen. (*She attempts to sit, realises she cannot and stands nonchalantly at the side of her chair.*) But I think I shall stand for a while. I find standing quite beneficial to my… posture!

GWENDOLEN: Indeed, Cecily, now that I look at you, I find your posture to be remarkably upright… I may try this… standing… for a while (*crosses back to table, knocks back her wine*) but not just now. (*Sits down abruptly, getting a little tipsy.*)

MERRIMAN: (*Staggers in with a tray, CECILY hands him the carafe.*) You rang? Or have my ears gone again?

CECILY: Some more white wine, Merriman, please.

MERRIMAN bows and goes to exit, but stops as CECILY drops the cane with a thump.

MERRIMAN: (*Confused, looking at the carafe in his hand.*) What did I drop? Er… (*Looking around at the ground frantically.*)

GWENDOLEN: What was that?

CECILY: (*Sings loudly.*) Ladedadedadeda! I so love the dance…

CECILY shuffles around, trying to lift the cane, with her back to GWENDOLEN. MERRIMAN obligingly turns and winds up the gramophone, providing music for the dance he expects.

MERRIMAN: Oh, yes, it's that time, isn't it, Miss Cecily? Music and dance, music and dance…

Cecily proceeds to dance frantically around, then shoves the cane into MERRIMAN's hand. He looks at it, looks at GWENDOLEN, gasps and shoves it back to her. There are one or two more passings over of the cane.

CECILY: (*Managing to place the cane Upstage of the gramophone table, to MERRIMAN, whispering.*) Stop it! (*Waving at the gramophone, he gazing at her blankly.*). Stop it, Merriman... (*He turns off the phonograph.*) Go on, go on, shooooo!! (*MERRIMAN leaves huffily, walking Offstage in entirely the wrong direction for the house, then turning back, shaking his head.*)

MERRIMAN: (*Returning to go in the right direction.*) Music, then no music, tea, then wine, then more wine... I don't know... I don't know at all... this is beyond me... (*He exits Stage Right again.*)

GWENDOLEN: (*Turning to look at her, shocked.*) My dear girl! You must not perform these... contortions... in front of the servants! I fear they may become disturbed, and might even revolt! Kindly contain yourself, Cecily! (*Turns back to face audience.*)

CECILY: Thank you Gwendolen, I do become a little carried away from time to time with my ... artistic endeavours!

The two women sit in silence for a moment, CECILY tentatively reaching across and taking her glass of wine, sipping it. Silence. Birdsong.

CECILY: It is so nice to just sit and do nothing, is it not, Gwendolen?

GWENDOLEN: Doing nothing is the prerogative of the working classes, dear.

MERRIMAN enters with another carafe of white wine and delivers it to the table, CECILY reaching to take it from him before he drops it.

MERRIMAN: (*Disgustedly*) More Hock!

CECILY: Thank you, Merriman, that will be all. (*He puts his hands on his knees and puffs for a few seconds, then creaks off.*)

CECILY: Oh, but I am always busy... I find that lately my days run by in a haze of creativity, what with my pottery and my painting and my dance and my ladies' séances and my meditations... I hardly have time to think!

GWENDOLEN: (*Finishing her wine, CECILY pouring them both another.*) Cecily?

CECILY: Yes, Gwendolen?

GWENDOLEN: I do sometimes wonder…

CECILY: Wonder what, dear Gwendolen?

GWENDOLEN: What they… think about…

CECILY: (*Puzzled*) Who, dear?

GWENDOLEN: Men. Not all men, you understand, not the great unwashed, but… our men. Our Ernests. What DO they think about?

CECILY: (*Amused*) Why don't you ask your Ernest, dear? He might surprise you with an honest answer, you know…

GWENDOLEN: I hardly think it appropriate for a wife to ask her husband such an… intimate question. It might lead to all sorts of unwanted honesty and soul baring, which would be detrimental to any relationship…

CECILY: I believe in the importance of being honest, in life and in a marriage. I fully understand my Ernest's mind! There is not, I have to say, a great deal in it, but that suits me very well… to my poor poor Miss Prism's disappointment, I am not a great intellectual… but I understand my Ernest's little ways, and that suits us admirably… (*Looking shrewdly at GWENDOLEN.*) For example, I understand when Ernest needs to stay in town… alone… to spend some time with his friends, and indeed I find it wonderfully refreshing to have some time to myself!

GWENDOLEN: I can see how time without Algy is desirable…

CECILY: (*Interrupting quite forcefully.*) I understand (*Again a glance at G*) that sometimes a man can… tire of the rigid routine of a parliamentary role, and might long for the simple bucolic pleasures of his past life. We are so free here in the country, unbound by the restrictions of city living. We are free to dance and cavort with the children, to paint, and sing, and… (*Waving her wineglass around*) simply… be!

GWENDOLEN: All very well for you, dear girl. We who live in the public eye must have higher standards. Indeed your Ernest, my little Algy of yore, was never the brightest of lights in terms of career… I am sure the House is relieved at his many absences in the country… Not so MY Ernest, whose dedication to duty and attendance at the House is exemplary... so much so that I... hardly ever see him lately... (*She almost breaks down, catches herself, takes some more wine.*)

CECILY: Dear Gwendolen! (*She reaches over and takes GWENDOLEN's hand, GWENDOLEN allows her.*) And does that... does your Ernest's absence... distress you?

GWENDOLEN: It... pains me greatly to say... it does, Cecily, it does! (*Starts to cry, finds a hankie in her bag and blows her nose.*) I never thought I could be so... affected by a man, I must confess!

CECILY: Affected? By your husband? In what way?

GWENDOLEN: I do not know... I have given my life to him and... my every effort since our marriage has been simply to ensure the smooth running of his existence. Why, he never even saw our children until 6.30 every evening when they were little, and even then for 10 minutes only, lest they weary him. And now that they are old enough to sit at table with us, I only allow them to speak to him when they are spoken to, although of late that rule has been more and more difficult to apply... my little family seem to be able to carry on a conversation without MY help at all! And Augusta... well, I do not know what my daughter does, she absents herself from home so frequently and without permission... I cannot imagine where she goes on such occasions... she has refused several promising introductions to Young Tories... refused them!... Oh, Cecily, this... new century, this new world that people speak of, I fear it is already beyond me, and all, all is slipping out of control! I no longer know... what my position is!

CECILY: You have a most important position, dearest! That of the beloved wife of your Ernest, dear, you must believe that!

GWENDOLEN: All middle-aged men believe that THEY are loved. That's their tragedy. No middle-aged woman does. That's hers.

CECILY: My poor, Gwendolen! Our husbands do still love us, I am sure of it!

GWENDOLEN: I wish I could be so sure. Of late, I fear all of Ernest's absences are not... not what they seem.

CECILY: What do you mean?

GWENDOLEN: I mean that Ernest… I fear he has been lying to me, Cecily!

CECILY: Lying? My Uncle Jack?

GWENDOLEN: I really wish you would not continue to call him that, Cecily! His name, and not as in your Ernest's case by an impulsive christening, is Ernest and has been from birth!

CECILY: I'm sorry, Gwendolen, truly! But I don't believe… even if your Ernest is lying, it's probably for the most… upright and innocent of reasons, and signifies nothing!

GWENDOLEN: I believe of course that every marriage requires a degree of deception to survive… but I suspect… (*She breaks down again.*)

CECILY: What do you suspect, Gwendolen?

GWENDOLEN: (*Pulling herself together.*) I suspect there is… another woman!

CECILY: No! There isn't! (*She stands, distractedly kicking the cane and picking it up, along with a spade which has been lying against the plinth.*)

GWENDOLEN: (*Surprised*) You seem so certain, dear! But I'm afraid I have examined every possible reason for Ernest's unexplained absences, which grow longer and longer as time passes, and that is the only conclusion possible. What else could tempt him away from the delights of our perfect home?

CECILY: (*Coming to a decision and holding the cane out to let GWENDOLEN see it.*) But Gwendolen… perhaps the delights of home are… not quite enough? Perhaps… Uncle J… your Ernest… would prefer a somewhat – simpler – life?

GWENDOLEN: (*Pause.*) What is that?

CECILY: (*Looking at the spade wonderingly.*) I have no idea!!

GWENDOLEN: What is that object which you are holding in your RIGHT hand? That object which I believe to be a cane belonging to – my Ernest! You! Deceitful wretch!

CECILY: Gwendolen! How dare you!

GWENDOLEN: You are the temptress who has been luring my Ernest away from me! I knew from the moment we met that we were destined to be enemies! No woman should make a friend of a female who is pretty. I demand that you show me that cane at once!

CECILY: (*Reluctantly holding the cane out.*) Very well, Gwendolen, but I must assure you this is not what you think it is…

GWENDOLEN: (*Snatching the cane from her.*) I think it is a cane, Cecily. I think it is a cane belonging to my husband, Ernest. I think it is a cane left here by my husband Ernest, on a visit of some… immoral nature!

CECILY: (*Snatching the cane back.*) How can you have such a low opinion, both of your dear husband, and indeed of me, Gwendolen! He was my guardian! You cannot leap to conclusions in this manner!

GWENDOLEN: (*Snatching it back again.*) I do not leap, Cecily, I ascend.

CECILY: (*Indicating their seats.*) Please, dear Gwendolen, sit down.

GWENDOLEN: (*Sitting.*) I await your explanation, since you seem entirely convinced both of your own innocence and that of Ernest. Pray enlighten me at once!

CECILY: You are very agitated. I promise I can explain everything, but you must promise me to be calm…

GWENDOLEN: (*Waving the cane at her violently.*) I am the very soul of calm! My stoicism in the face of trouble is legendary! I have survived many domestic calamities with perfect equilibrium, and shall continue to do so… now kindly explain, Cecily!

CECILY: (*Sitting down, whipping the cane from GWENDOLEN and clasping it to her bosom.*) Some time last year… I believe it was just after Uncle Jack had had his Public Transport Bill passed…

GWENDOLEN: (*Through gritted teeth.*) Ernest! Ernest! Ernest! He has never been Jack, and never will be.

CECILY: Ernest then! I am sorry, Gwendolen, but to me he will always be my gentle and loving Uncle Jack, who delighted so much in his life here that even though he had found love in London, he spent many happy days... escaping the hurly burly –

GWENDOLEN: *(Interrupting.)* Hurly burly?

CECILY: His words, not mine, dear. He has always felt at home here, and lately... well, lately he has felt the need to... escape every now and then, to come... home... and fall back into the easy world of our little estate... to play cricket with my Ernest and some of the village lads on the green, to sit in the garden and read, and to walk the lanes in the summer and sit by the fire in the winter. To debate with the girls on the Cause. Why, to live simply, as he put it.

GWENDOLEN: To live simply, Cecily? I have never heard such nonsense! If everyone were to... live simply... how would the world go on? And I am shocked to think that you and Algernon have kept this from me. What is this... Cause??? And who are these... girls ... of whom you speak? What harpies have you introduced him to?

CECILY: Your daughter and mine, dear friend. Augusta and Jemima. Two modern young women who seek their rightful place in a world dominated by men. (*Going Up Stage Right to fetch pamphlets.*) We should be proud of our little history makers. Of our little suffragists.

GWENDOLEN: (*Aghast.*) My Augusta a Suffragist? Mama would turn in her grave at the thought... our girls have joined this – deplorable movement to defeminise women? I cannot believe it. And I cannot believe my Ernest would ever allow it!

CECILY: Do you not think it a compliment to you, my dear Gwendolen, that Ernest believes women to be capable of determining their own lives?

GWENDOLEN: I... do not know, Cecily, how to interpret his actions. He is aware, I believe, of my opinion on the Suffragists... that this movement will only result in deep unhappiness for women, in enslavement to a life of... drudgery both outside the home and in it, to a diminution of the position of the woman in the home, and ultimately to the breakdown of Society as we know it!

CECILY: Ah. Perhaps that is why he has not been honest about his conversations with our girls. He knew you would not approve. But,

Gwendolen, this movement can lead to the betterment of all women's lives, I truly believe that!

GWENDOLEN: My life requires no betterment, thank you!

CECILY: (*Stands and walks Downstage.*) When Jemima first came to me, to confess her involvement in the cause, your Augusta had come to stay for the weekend, and they were both so… impassioned, so utterly convinced of the rightness of the movement, I believe I was a little swept away. It seems Augusta first converted, as she put it, after a meeting with Mrs Pankhurst.

GWENDOLEN: (*Shocked.*) Mrs… that Bolshevik she-devil? No, no, no, not my little Augusta… she could not… she would not be drawn in by such a dangerous woman!

CECILY: Whatever your opinion of Mrs Pankhurst, my dear, she is a strong and intelligent woman, and a wonderful example for many young women. Perhaps to our view of the world, she is extreme, but sometimes extremity is necessary to bring about change… has history not always shown us this?… At any rate, Augusta had brought some literature for Jemima to read. They showed it to me, and in the course of our discussions that afternoon, I came to realise that I – and indeed most women of our generation – had been living a sort of half-life, depending on our men to regulate our existence, with no voice whatsoever for the betterment of our lot, or indeed the lot of those poor women who toil in factories and other dreadful places.

GWENDOLEN: If these – women – choose to enter the world of men, they must take the consequences! Better they stay in their homes and be ruler of their own domain than plunge themselves into lives better suited to the male of the species!

CECILY: But they have no choice, dear friend. Nowadays many women are forced out of the home and into places of toil out of necessity. For them, it is work or starve, and watch their children starving. And still they have no power over their own destiny. (*She moves Upstage to GWENDOLEN.*) Nor indeed, dear Gwendolen, have we. I came to see that even though I manage this estate, from the household to the gardens and the worker's cottages, the occupants of those cottages, by virtue of being male, possess a right denied to me, simply because I am a woman. I confess I was moved to a degree of passion which almost matched Jemima's!

GWENDOLEN: Passion is most unattractive in an older woman! Women of our class have no place in such a movement, Cecily!

CECILY: We are the very class who can try to change things, Gwendolen! The only class that Parliament will hear! That afternoon the girls were leaving to attend a rally, and I rushed upstairs to change my clothing, wondering what would be appropriate to wear to such an occasion... and I thought about painting some placards expounding our views...

GWENDOLEN: (*Interrupting, ignoring CECILY's obvious distress.*) I am surprised at a woman of your years and experience being... seduced by these fanatical women – women who are prepared to kill themselves under a horse for... what? To live in a man's world? Oh, Cecily, this is dangerous nonsense!

CECILY: (*Vehemently.*) Dangerous perhaps, but never nonsense, Gwendolen! (*She moves Upstage Right of the plinth, visibly upset. GWENDOLEN, shocked, attempts to regain solid ground.*)

GWENDOLEN: What is of much more importance to me is that I find it deeply sad that Ernest would not feel... able to confide in me... (*Suddenly turning to CECILY*) But why does he come here, to your home?

CECILY: He comes here for a little peace, Gwendolen, that is all. A little peace and the opportunity to be alone with his thoughts, not to be regimented into doing every moment of every day!

GWENDOLEN: (*Turning to glare at CECILY.*) Regimented? Are you suggesting, Cecily, that I have been guilty of regimenting my dear Ernest? I have always allowed Ernest time to himself... from six to half past on every second Monday, and from three to four on Sundays... Mama would never have allowed such liberty to a husband. Why, my poor father was often found in later years in the stables, communicating with the grooms, as a means of escape from...

CECILY: Ah... from Lady Bracknell??

GWENDOLEN: Oh dear. Oh dear, Cecily! Have I... have I become my own mother?

CECILY: All women become like their mothers...

GWENDOLEN: What a tragedy!

CECILY: (*Turning to her, eagerly.*) But it need not be a tragedy, dearest Gwendolen! I am ignorant of my similarities to my mother, but I believe... (*Taking GWENDOLEN's hand*) I really believe that once one becomes aware of a... fault, or problem in one's life, or in one's relationship... that one is halfway to remedying or solving it! If you would only join me in the meditation taught by Monsieur Coué.

GWENDOLEN: Meditation! Now I am to become a monk, am I? And a French one at that?

CECILY: He is an aristrocrat, even if only a French one... I believe his philosophy could change your life so easily, Gwendolen! And I believe, if we are to be truly honest with ourselves, dearest, we both may need to change our lives! You see, Gwendolen, on the day I told you about... when I came downstairs to go to their rally with them, they... they had already left... they had forgotten about me. I was... superfluous to their needs, or the needs of those who fight for the cause. (*She turns to look at GWENDOLEN.*) For the first time I realised... Our moment is gone, Gwendolen. It is time to hand over the reins to our daughters.

GWENDOLEN: Has it come to that already, Cecily?

CECILY: I'm afraid so.

GWENDOLEN: I do believe Mama held on to the reins, as you call them, until her death.

CECILY: She was a... (*Catches herself, changes what she was going to say*) strong and wonderful woman. In the manner of her time...

GWENDOLEN: Do we allow ourselves to be discarded so early, then?

CECILY: (*Taking GWENDOLEN's hand.*) Perhaps we should view it as a good thing! Perhaps this is an opportunity to – live one's own life!

GWENDOLEN: If by 'living one's own life' you mean being condemned to dancing naked by the lake and straining to hear spirit voices, I think I would rather live someone else's! Do you wish to… dance into the sunset, inebriated? Or spend your time on the frivolous pursuit of art?

CECILY: (*Haughtily.*) You do not understand, Gwendolen, what a consolation the arts can be!

GWENDOLEN: (*Nodding.*) Consolation. Indeed. For what, exactly?

CECILY: (*Flustered.*) Perhaps consolation is the wrong word…

GWENDOLEN: (*Gently taking her hand.*) I do not think so, dear. For all your protestations of peace and happiness, what I see before me is a woman abandoned by her husband – Algernon was always a flibbertigibbet – and discarded by her children, filling her days with frippery and (*picking up the carafe*) inappropriate comforts!

CECILY: (*Defensively taking the wine back.*) No! I mean… I only ordered some wine to soothe your distress, dearest! I never… well, I very seldom…

GWENDOLEN: Where is your vaunted honesty now?

CECILY: (*Sits back suddenly, defeated*). Perhaps you are right. But what else is there for us, Gwendolen? How are we to live?

GWENDOLEN: With dignity, little one. Dignity and good corsetry are the only refuge of the older woman. (*Sarcastically.*) I wonder if our daughters' Cause will challenge that in any way?

CECILY: Perhaps not for us, dear Gwendolen. But in the future… (*Suddenly animated.*) Only think what women might achieve if they were allowed to become the architects of their own destiny!

GWENDOLEN: I believe I have always been the architect of my own destiny, Cecily. I acknowledge that there may be other women who are in need of some degree of control in their lives. As to the Cause, I hope that you are right, for our sakes and for the lives of future women. But for now, my dear, I think that it may be appropriate for you to find an occupation more… suited to your station than that of dancing monk!

CECILY: (*Giggles.*) Dancing monk indeed! You and I, dear friend, are mirrors for each other - you with your soirées and charities, and I with my arts and crafts, while the real world moves on, leaving us behind!

GWENDOLEN: The real world may try as it might, dearest, but I for one will not be left behind. Come, come, little Cecily, you are made of sterner stuff than that! Our daughters may find new ways to live their lives, but we, and other women of our class, must live as examples to the lower orders.

CECILY: As examples to all women, Gwendolen. All women…

GWENDOLEN: (*Suddenly deciding.*) You must come to London, Cecily. You must forget this rural nonsense and open up your lovely town house – I believe Algernon lives in two rooms like a rat and keeps the rest shut up – it is such a waste to see a home like that unlived in! Only think of the soirées you might give, the at homes, the balls – the introductions we might make for Augusta and Jemima!!!

CECILY: (*Thinking.*) A waste… indeed. (*Slowly.*) You have opened my eyes, but not to the delights of a London Season. I have been blind, but now, thanks to our wonderful meeting of minds, I can finally see! I know now what my path is, Gwendolen, and I thank you for showing it to me!

GWENDOLEN: You do? I did? Really? Quite. (*Totally bewildered.*) As I have said on many occasions, I knew from the moment we met that we were destined to become the greatest of friends.

CECILY: Oh, I am glad of that, Gwendolen! I shall come to you in London, but only until my house is fully opened. Thereafter I shall divide my time between it and this lovely rural retreat of ours, bringing with me those poor females who have suffered for the Cause, who have been jailed and brutalised, so that they may recover and re-enter the fray!

GWENDOLEN: (*Horrified.*) Use your house as a… oh good Lord, what have I… they will steal the silver, Cecily! They will pilfer their criminal way through your home and leave you with nothing of value! (*Pulling herself together.*) Really, dear? Surely you would better serve your daughter by introducing her to good society and helping her to make a match?

CECILY: And condemn her to a life such as ours, Gwendolen? A life of… making do, of taking second best, of… filling our days with frippery until we die? No, Gwendolen, better my daughter witnesses me fight for her rights than dance myself into the sunset.

GWENDOLEN: (*Admiringly and a little shocked.*) And I opened your eyes to this? Indeed… I am glad to have been of such assistance, dear little Cecily. Glad and a little shaken at the violence of your convictions…

CECILY: True convictions sentence us to action!

GWENDOLEN: … and sometimes to a prison, Cecily!

CECILY: Physical imprisonment is nothing compared to a lack of mental freedom!

GWENDOLEN: (*Caught up in CECILY's passion.*) How swiftly the world changes! Are women supposed now to have convictions? I thought that was a male prerogative, although I have seen very few men express convictions they would act upon, most being delivered from their armchairs by the fire… I wonder if I might somehow manage to develop some convictions myself?

CECILY: I am sure you could! We may all change, once we have found the honesty to admit the need!

GWENDOLEN: What a strange world we live in! I… hesitate to admit defeat, but I'm afraid in this case I must! I do not know how to… change!

CECILY: Perhaps with tiny steps, some change may be achieved, Gwendolen! For instance, why not… talk to Augusta about her political activities?

GWENDOLEN: Perhaps you are right… (*Takes the pamphlet with distaste*) and… perhaps I could let Ernest out on a longer leash than that which I currently employ… perhaps he might even shortly think of – (*a bit horrified at the thought*) retiring from political life! But what would he do with his time? And what would I do with him? Good Lord, would he wish to spend more time with me? (*Panicking a bit.*)

CECILY: There is no need to worry. He simply needs to spend more time communing with nature.

GWENDOLEN: Communing with nature! (*Placing cane behind chair.*) How peaceful you make it all sound! I was of the impression that nature was red in tooth and claw, but obviously one should never take a poet at his word... However, to each his own, Cecily. (*Pushing pamphlet across table.*)

CECILY: (*Ruefully.*) I should love to know that my little life has made a difference in the lives of others, and I truly believe the Cause is the way!

GWENDOLEN: (*Unconvinced.*) Hmmmmmm...

CECILY: I was so terrified of the thought at first, but then I began to use the method of Monsieur Coué –

GWENDOLEN: Oh, is the French monk back again? He is such a fad in London...

CECILY: Oh, but Gwendolen! Perhaps it would help you to use it?... every evening, just before bedtime, or first thing in the morning, you repeat over and over – I do it at least ten times – 'every day, in every way, I'm getting better and better'.

GWENDOLEN: I see no need to tell myself something which I know already, Cecily! (*CECILY, offended, moves Up tage Left. GWENDOLEN sighs heavily and looks miserable. She then tries to repair the rift.*)... Besides, I have nothing to wear that is purple, green and white – what a horrid combination of colours!

CECILY: (*Eager to reconcile.*) Indeed. You would be loathe to offend your seamstress with such a colour scheme...

GWENDOLEN: ... and if I haven't got the appropriate clothing to attend... meetings and rallies...

CECILY: Precisely. You couldn't presume to appear without being correctly attired, could you?

GWENDOLEN: Absolutely not. I wouldn't feel...

BOTH: Right.

CECILY: But I would, Gwendolen! Perhaps when you have had a little more time to reflect on it, you will see the worthiness of the Cause we fight for, I and your daughter and mine. I shall wear the sash with pride and play my part in history with joy!

GWENDOLEN: Hmmmm. So long as the sash is worn over a decent corset… (*Taking a pocket watch out of her handbag and checking it.*) And now, Cecily, I must leave you… I am organising another soirée for tomorrow night, and I must speak to Ernest about not staying late in the House, for he will disrupt my entire programme if he is not home by… (*She stops abruptly and looks at CECILY, aghast.*) Oh dear, Cecily! Off I go again!

CECILY: Gradual change, dearest. Small steps every day and gradually our lives will have transformed into something – quite … beautiful in every way!

GWENDOLEN: (*Smiling and embracing her, holding her at arm's length.*) Dear little one! Until we meet again! (*She turns to leave – as the lights go down.*) Every day, in – what, dear?

CECILY: In every way, I'm getting… (*Handing Gwendolen the cane.*)

BOTH: Better and better.

Lights down.

THE END

The Quiet Land
Malachy McKenna

First produced in Bewley's Café Theatre in August 2015.

DIRECTOR: Bairbre Ní Chaoimh
STAGE MANAGER: Helena White
SET DESIGNER: Andy Murray
LIGHTING DESIGNER: Colm Maher
COSTUME DESIGNER: Miriam Duffy
PHOTOGRAPHY: Futoshi Sakauchi

CHARACTERS & CAST:

EAMON McCONNELL (*elderly farmer*): Derry Power
NASHEE (Ignatious) FINN (*elderly farmer*): Des Keogh

—

Malachy McKenna is a member of the Writers Guild of Ireland. He trained as an actor at the Focus Stanislavski Studio, Dublin, under the late Deirdre O'Connell. His first stage play, *Tillsonburg*, premiered at the Focus Theatre and won the Stewart Parker Literary Trust Award. It subsequently had several Irish tours and had its North American premiere with the Canadian Stage Company, Toronto, and has played in Rep in Arad State Theatre, Romania, on numerous occasions. *The Quiet Land*, first written for radio, was a Gold Medal winner with RTÉ for Best Radio Drama at the World Festival of Radio in New York in July, 2015, having previously been awarded the P.J. O'Connor Award in 2014. The stage adaptation of *The Quiet Land*, having premiered at Bewley's, has toured to critical acclaim through Ireland and Scotland.

Setting: An old wooden stile on a hillside. The stile also serves as a seat.

The action takes place over the course of a morning and afternoon.

SOUND: The second verse of The Corries version of 'The Quiet Land of Erin' fades and blends into sound of sheep and crows.

Lights up on NASHEE (Nay-Shee) at the fence. He carries a billhook and stares up the hill. He makes several moves to head up the hill but changes his mind. He's uncomfortable. Suddenly he sees someone coming and begins tapping the gate with the billhook. EAMON arrives, limping, using a hurl as a crutch. His head is heavily bandaged. Large binoculars hang round his neck. Nearby stands a full bag of turf, an old rusted milk churn and a tree stump.

EAMON: Have you nare a sledge?

NASHEE: Huh?

EAMON: You'll have your eye out with that billhook.

NASHEE: Eamon!

EAMON: Nashee!

NASHEE: I saw the auld stile was falling asunder when I got up here. And the fence down. I'm doing a patch up job.

EAMON: With a billhook! Are ya mad? Here, let me give it a few whacks with this hurl. (*EAMON wallops a few lats in the stile.*)

NASHEE: So?

EAMON: So.

NASHEE: They let you out?

EAMON: They did. Good behaviour.

NASHEE: I saw the ambulance going down the lane yesterday evening.

EAMON: They dropped me home in it. They're not supposed to do that you know. Said I was a special case.

NASHEE: You're that alright. They didn't give you a crutch?

EAMON: Ah, I prefer this auld hurl. More used to it. (*He takes a few swings of the hurl.*)

SOUND: Wild geese honking as they fly overhead, with the sound of crows blending in underneath.

NASHEE: Uh huh, there's the geese flying down to the lake. Winter is here.

EAMON: Yeah. D'ya see the way the crows nested lower this year in the ringfort beyond? A bad sign. A hard winter coming I'd say.

NASHEE: Twill soon be christmas Eamon.

EAMON: Aye. I suppose it will.

NASHEE: How long were you in there for at all?

EAMON: Well sure, over a month anyway.

NASHEE: And what way are ya now?

EAMON: Bit stiff is all. I have to do these exercises the physio one gave me.

NASHEE: And your head? You still have a bandage on?

EAMON: Well, twas a big cut.

NASHEE: Was it?

EAMON: Doctors said the head was split wide open. One ear to the other.

NASHEE: I'm awful sorry that happened you Eamon.

EAMON: Sure Jasus what are you sorry about?

NASHEE: I'm just saying like.

EAMON: Did I see the post van below in your yard this morning?

NASHEE: No.

EAMON: Who was it drove in?

NASHEE: Nobody.

EAMON: I saw the post van?

NASHEE: No. You didn't.

EAMON: Look it, I definitely saw the post van in your yard! (*He takes out his binoculars and looks through them.*)

NASHEE: No. No post today. (*A beat.*) Where did you get the fancy yokamebobs?

EAMON: The binoculars? One of the nurses bought 'em for me before I came home. Feckin' dear yokes so they are.

NASHEE: What did you get 'em for?

EAMON: For looking at stuff of course! What d'you think I got 'em for?

NASHEE: What was the nurse like?

EAMON: Alright, I suppose. Foreign. Hadn't a clue what she was saying half the time.

NASHEE: I heard twas touch and go with ya in there for a while.

EAMON: Did you now?

NASHEE: I thought I was going to have to iron a shirt.

EAMON: Huh! A rare event!

NASHEE: (*Gesturing to the turf.*) Mind you, I wound up having to iron one anyway.

EAMON: Poor auld Martin wha? His bag of turf still here. (*EAMON handles the turf.*) Good black turf too.

NASHEE: You missed the funeral.

EAMON: Don't I know that! Jasus. How could I have gone?

NASHEE: That's right. That's right. Of course. Of course.

EAMON: He went quick in the finish.

NASHEE: Poor auld frigger.

EAMON: Was he complaining at all?

NASHEE: Was he ever doing anything else? But no; there wasn't a bother on him.

EAMON: And what happened him at all?

NASHEE: They say twas his heart.

EAMON: That was always a weakness in the MacBriens. Remember auld Albert, the uncle, came back from England that time, keeled over snaggin' turnips on the hill?

NASHEE: God be good to him.

EAMON: Died in Brannigan's, I heard. Martin?

NASHEE: He did. Tripped going into the lounge. That was it. Well, it looked like he tripped. They say he was gone before he hit the ground.

EAMON: Are you sure it wasn't coming out of the lounge he tripped?

NASHEE: Now now Eamon! I know he was fond of it, but! Don't be tryin' to incinerate that he was… twas his heart that did for him!

EAMON: Did you stick your head in above while I was away?

NASHEE: Ah! I didn't like to. Did they mess the place up on ya?

EAMON: They did. (*A beat.*) The pint is bad in Brannigan's since Johnjoe Ryan sold it.

NASHEE: Tis. Tis. It is. You're right! Bad pint there now. Do you know what Martin said they were charging him for a glass of wine? Eight euro!

The Quiet Land

EAMON: Eight euro! Lord almighty! What was he doing drinking wine?

NASHEE: Sure he was off the drink. Red wine. That's what he drank when he was on the dry.

EAMON: Maybe that's what killed him.

NASHEE: How long is Johnjoe dead now?

EAMON: Must be ten years?

NASHEE: You could eat your dinner off the floor when he had the place. Kitty was a hoor with the mop.

EAMON: She was. Mind you, she was that without the mop. (*They share a laugh.*) Betty Brannigan now; she wouldn't be the cleanest. Who was she again?

NASHEE: She was… Betty Torpey as was, from beyond Killraddin; Mick Torpey was her father; used to take the horse and cart to the creamery years ago; hurled corner forward for Linbeg.

EAMON: Can't place him.

NASHEE: Jasus you can! He had a sister that was a dwarf!

EAMON: A dwarf!

NASHEE: Yeah. Remember her, Midgee they used to call her! She was always knitting in mass.

EAMON: Oh Mickey Torpey! Not Mick. Mickey! A sniggy little hurler, hard as a feckin bag of onions. Yeah. Jasus. The horse and cart wha. (*EAMON attempts to light a cigarette.*)

NASHEE: Them cigarettes will kill ya.

EAMON: They can join the queue! Feck it. I suppose you're right. (*He begrudgingly puts the cigarette back in the box.*) What ever happened the sister? The dwarf.

NASHEE: Not a whole lot. She didn't get any taller anyway. Wound up in a home in the end. She died, I suppose.

EAMON: The home is no way to finish up.

NASHEE: Sure, there's pros and cons for, and there's pros and cons against.

EAMON: What the hell do you mean by that?

NASHEE: Well –

EAMON: Well what? Don't tell me you want to wind up in the home?

NASHEE: I dunno. There's a lot to be said for it. Three meals a day. Television. Heat. Warm bed. Hot shower.

EAMON: Feckin' showers. That's what's giving everyone all the colds.

NASHEE: Nice nurses tucking you in.

EAMON: Tucking you in, me arse. There was no shortage of nurses where I'm after coming from and there was no tucking in, I can tell ya. You go in that door, you only come out the one way.

NASHEE: What's the alternative for us, would you mind telling me?

EAMON: What are we talking about all this for?

NASHEE: I dunno. Listen, about the post van… (*Their conversation overlaps.*)

EAMON: Oh yeah. Brannigan's! We were saying Betty is a dirty…

NASHEE: … maybe you were right.

EAMON: What? What are you saying?

NASHEE: Nothing. Here, give us a go of them binoculars.

EAMON: What?

NASHEE: Give us a look through 'em. (*EAMON hands them over. NASHEE tries to look through them the wrong way around.*)

EAMON: No, no, the other way round. (*NASHEE adjusts them and looks through the correct end.*) Pull them in to fit your eyes. From the side. Press down on them and they'll move in.

NASHEE: I can't see anything.

EAMON: Here, turn that little wheel in the middle; that's the focuser yoke.

NASHEE: Which way do I turn it? (*NASHEE drops the binoculars.*)

EAMON: Jasus, will you mind them, ya plike ya!

NASHEE: Sorry.

EAMON: Nearly a hundred feckin' euro and you bouncing 'em off the ground.

NASHEE: A hundred euro for them binoculars.

EAMON: Yeah!

NASHEE: They saw you coming!

EAMON: Huh ho! Aren't we the witty man today! Ah Jasus, me hip, here pick 'em up for me, will ya? I can't bend down! (*NASHEE hands him the binoculars.*) Ahh, Christ almighty. (*EAMON coughs violently.*)

NASHEE: Are you alright?

EAMON: No I'm not alright! (*A beat.*) I'm fine! I'm fine. (*EAMON examines the binoculars for damage.*)

NASHEE: Do they still work?

EAMON: Just about. (*Looks through the binoculars.*) Tell me, what's happenin' Martin's place now?

NASHEE: He left it to the sister beyond.

EAMON: Bridget. In America?

NASHEE: Yeah. She's the only one left. He shoulda got married years ago when he had the chance. No more than yourself.

EAMON: Will you leave me alone! Bad enough you annoyin' me! Did she even come home for the funeral? Bridget.

NASHEE: Oh she did! The little Yank husband with her. Dudley, he's called.

EAMON: Dudley!

NASHEE: Yeah. Dudley. You were great with her one time, weren't ya?

EAMON: I was not!

NASHEE: Oh. I thought that you and Bridget were…

EAMON: Me and Bridget were never anything! (*A beat.*) How did she look anyway?

NASHEE: Looked right well. Big long coat on her. She was all dolled up.

EAMON: I bet she was, and she getting her claws into thirty acres.

NASHEE: There was people nearer than America didn't go to the funeral at all.

EAMON: I couldn't go, could I? Between me head and me hip! And I laid up in hospital!

NASHEE: Sure I know that, Eamon. I didn't mean you!

EAMON: I suppose they were all talking about me? At the funeral. Were they?

NASHEE: Well, sure, the day that was in it, I don't think your name came up.

EAMON: No! I bet ya it didn't. And me after having the daylights kicked outa me, in me own feckin' house! D'ya know how many visitors I had in hospital?

NASHEE: Sure I had no way of getting to ya. You know I failed the eye…

EAMON: I know all about your eyesight and your driving licence! One visitor is all I had. One visitor!

NASHEE: I know.

EAMON: What do you mean you know?

NASHEE: I knew Martin went in to see ya.

EAMON: Why didn't you come?

NASHEE: Ah, I didn't like to see you like that. I prefer to remember you the way you were.

EAMON: What are you talking about? Amn't I still here! Jasus Christ you have me dead before I'm even gone!

NASHEE: Ah, you know what I mean. I was sorry I didn't go with Martin after. He got a grand haircut in town – seven euro.

EAMON: Jasus. Cheaper than a wine in Brannigan's.

NASHEE: He looked right well at the team of fifty-nine reunion. Martin did. You missed that too.

EAMON: I know!

NASHEE: Twas a great night. Martin was in flying form, God be good to him.

EAMON: Were you at it?

NASHEE: I went with Martin. Did you not see his photo in the *Gazette*?

EAMON: No! (*NASHEE carefully produces a newspaper cutting and unfolds it.*)

NASHEE: I kept the page. Look at him there! Your old midfield partner wha? Hard to think he'd be a goner only a week later.

EAMON: That's you beside him!

NASHEE: Well spotted! Yeah. That's me. At the top table if you don't mind!

EAMON: The top table? You weren't even on the team in fifty-nine.

NASHEE: Oh, I think I was. I think I got a run out.

EAMON: You no more got a run out than… Bab Lawlor's ass.

NASHEE: Well, Father Meara said seeing as how there was so many of the team, absent, it might look better if I took your place.

EAMON: You took my place!

NASHEE: Yeah. Sure twas only an auld evening out.

EAMON: And your face in the paper. Anything there about me being in hospital?

NASHEE: No.

EAMON: No. Might as well be dead.

NASHEE: Oh you were missed! Indeed'n you were. How's Eamon McConnell a few of them asked me? They were all talking about the solo run you did to score the winning goal in the fifty-nine final.

EAMON: Who was talking about me?

NASHEE: Can't remember exactly. There was a fair few talking about you though.

EAMON: Fair few, me arse. You have a letter there I see.

NASHEE: What?

EAMON: I said I see you have a letter. Sticking outa your coat.

NASHEE: Oh yeah.

EAMON: I thought the post van didn't come today.

NASHEE: That's an auld letter I have for a while.

EAMON: Looks new enough to me. What is it?

NASHEE: Just an auld form, is all.

EAMON: Not from that official that was here last summer, is it?

NASHEE: Who?

EAMON: That bollox that came down from Dublin. In the jumper and the sandals; told us we couldn't cut any more turf below. What did he call the bog?

NASHEE: A special area of conservation. But sure you can put in for the compensation.

EAMON: What in the name of Jasus would I want to do that for? Get paid to sit on me arse when I could be out doing the turf in the fresh air? That's what has the country the way it is. Is that what your form is for – compensation?

NASHEE: No.

EAMON: Well, what is it then?

NASHEE: Tis nothing.

EAMON: How come you never got me to read it?

NASHEE: Why?

EAMON: Sure don't I read all the forms for you, with your feckin' eyesight.

NASHEE: Well, I managed this one myself! Can we leave it so?

EAMON: Fine! Fine! (*Under his breath*) Feckin' compensation…

NASHEE refolds the newspaper cutting and carefully puts it in his pocket. EAMON picks up a sod of turf.

NASHEE: He wasn't the worst of 'em, Martin.

EAMON: Indeed'n he wasn't.

NASHEE: And all the rows ye had. What were ye always arguing about?

EAMON: I don't know. Nothing, I suppose. Our last row was about me billhook. I thought he had it. But, now, I see tis you have it.

NASHEE: Sorry, Eamon. I thought twas mine. Twas in Martin's yard ages ago and I just grabbed it. Me auld eyes, you know.

EAMON: You see enough, I think.

NASHEE: What had Martin to say – when he came to see you?

EAMON: Not much. He hoped I'd get home soon. Didn't want to be stuck so far in off the road with just you for company.

NASHEE: Did they take much? When they robbed ya?

EAMON: Why?

NASHEE: No why.

EAMON: They took the bit of money I got for last summer's turf, from the cupboard behind the range.

NASHEE: Jasus, that's shocking.

EAMON: Funny though, they knew exactly what they were looking for, and where it was! Isn't that strange?

NASHEE: I suppose the guards have a few, whatyamacallems, leads?

EAMON: Leads! Are you joking me? They know as much about what's going on around here as, as, as, as… as a pig knows about baking a cake! The barracks is shut half the time, a timetable on the wall saying when they're available. Just to make sure the thugs know when to terrify us at their leisure!

NASHEE: Oh the guards knew they were about the place.

EAMON: What?

NASHEE: Paddy Divine saw them that day driving up the bog lane.

EAMON: Saw who?

NASHEE: The robbers! They had them ballyclava yokes on their faces. Paddy pulled across the lane in the jeep. And didn't he have the shotgun on the seat. So he phoned the guards, on the mobile, and says he, I'm here on the bog lane, with the gun beside me and a gang with ballyclavas is after going down past me in a van. I won't let them drive out, says he, until you get here.

EAMON: And what did the guards do?

NASHEE: You're not going to believe what he said to him.

EAMON: Who?

NASHEE: Tierney, the guard. You know him, redhead, awful young looking…

EAMON: I know him! What did he say?

NASHEE: Says he, and I'm only quoting what Paddy Divine told me, says he; the guard I mean, not Paddy…

EAMON: Will ya for Jasus sake tell me what he said!

NASHEE: Says he, 'Pull your jeep back off that lane immediately and let them go. We know who they are and they're heavily armed.'

EAMON: So he let them go!

NASHEE: He had to. Tierney said if he used the gun tis Paddy'd be in the wrong.

EAMON: And then they came to me.

NASHEE: That very same night.

EAMON: And the guards did nothing!

NASHEE: Well sure they're doing their best, I suppose. What can they do? Tis no picnic for them these days either.

EAMON: That's not my fault, is it?

NASHEE: No. You're probably safer not keeping money in the house.

EAMON: There was feck all to take only me bit of turf money! Why didn't they rob you, I wonder?

NASHEE: What'd make you say that?

EAMON: Maybe twas you they wanted to rob, and they got the wrong house! Sure everyone knows about your loose floorboard. Communion money probably still there.

NASHEE: There's nothing under my floorboard. Nuala had me put everything in the bank.

EAMON: Did she now? Well, isn't Nuala the cute little hoor? (*EAMON takes a small sod from Martin's bag of turf.*)

NASHEE: If you're going to talk about my niece like that, I'm going home.

EAMON: Ahh! Good black turf indeed. Martin always had good turf.

NASHEE: He always left a bag here.

EAMON: A bag for the bog he'd say. Good luck for the following year. (*He directs NASHEE into position in front of the stile.*) Stand in there.

NASHEE: What are you doing?

EAMON: That stile is the goals. Try and stop this cipín with the billhook.

NASHEE: Hold on! I'll take off me coat. And me hat. (*He hangs his coat on the fence and puts his glasses in a safe place.*)

EAMON: Are you ready?

NASHEE: Not too hard now.

EAMON: McConnell is on the twenty-one. The whistle's about to blow. Time is up. He bends. He rises it.

NASHEE: Wo! Wo!

EAMON: What?

NASHEE: You didn't bend, or rise it. Tis in your hand.

EAMON: Sure I can't bend with me… Jasus

NASHEE: Oh yeah. Sorry. What? Are you not going to hit it?

EAMON: Ah you're after taking the fecking good out of it now!

NASHEE: Go on and take the shot will you.

EAMON: The ball is in his hand! He strikes. (*EAMON whacks the cipín at NASHEE.*)

NASHEE: (*In his best Muircheartaigh commentary*) Saved! A great save by the mighty Ignatious Finn from the hill!

EAMON: Nothing wrong with your eyes there.

NASHEE: You probably took it easy on me. I saved the turf. D'you get it? Saved the turf! Ha ha.

EAMON: Very droll. (*He replaces the cipín of turf in the sack.*)

NASHEE: Did you hear our current crop of misfits lost to the Templecrory juniors?

EAMON: To the juniors! Arra for f… They're not training right! And they're not eating right, either. I see 'em on the bridge after mass, the few that still go that is! Sitting eating feckin' ice creams, syrup dripping off them that'd sit in your gut for a week. Whatever happened to bacon and cabbage? No one eats that anymore! Of course you can't get right bacon now, either. Little slivers of things on the pan now that you'd read the newspaper through. And then, when you're frying these yokes there's all this white stuff coming out of them. White stuff oozing out of the bacon! And you know what that is, of course?

NASHEE: No. What?

EAMON: Sure the feckin'pigs must be eating ice cream as well! (*They share a good laugh. EAMON looks through the binoculars.*)

SOUND: *Crows cawing.*

EAMON: Hey, where's the rest of the sheep? I only see Cleary's sheep. Where's Martin's sheep on the hill?

NASHEE: Sure they're gone.

EAMON: Gone where?

NASHEE: Bridget and the little Yank, Dudley, got rid of them. Sold them to a fella from Mayo.

EAMON: Sold them! That quick! And not even to a local.

NASHEE: Who was going to look after them?

EAMON: And the hill empty now!

1**NASHEE**: Well – that's another thing I heard.

EAMON: What?

NASHEE: Paddy Divine's youngest, Jennifer, she drives the scooter for the Cinnamon Schezwan.

EAMON: Drives the scooter?

NASHEE: Yeah, she does the deliveries.

EAMON: Christ Almighty! And all the schooling she got. Winds up driving a scooter!

NASHEE: Oh no, she's still at school. Won't be finished till next year. She's doing what they call... the transmission year.

EAMON: What's that?

NASHEE: Tis this new scheme they have, where they take a year off, and do whatever they like, to help 'em figure out what they want to do.

EAMON: A year off! To help 'em figure… Who pays for that?

NASHEE: I dunno. Comes out of somewhere, I suppose.

EAMON: By Jasus, tis well for 'em! And she's driving for who? The scooter.

NASHEE: The Cinnamon Schezwan, the big new Chinese restaurant, where the handball alley used to be. That's the in place now.

EAMON: Sure, that's more of it. God be with the handball alley. What are ya telling me all this for?

NASHEE: Didn't Jennifer see Bridget McBrien and the Yank husband having a big pow wow in the restaurant with yer man from Aurora.

EAMON: The windmill fella?

NASHEE: Wind energy, yeah. He had brochures all over the table. He paid for the dinners, spicy stuff; burn the mouth off you, Jennifer says. He paid for all the drinks too! Which is more than little Dudley did after Martin's funeral, I can tell ya. Yeah. That fella must have got a wallop off a cash register one time; he was very reluctant to stand too near it at the counter.

EAMON: They're letting that crowd in onto the hill!

NASHEE: Seemingly they're going to put a big wind 'turban' on it. A million euro each they cost.

EAMON: And all the times Martin told them where to go with their windmills! Wouldn't have them next nigh nor near the place.

NASHEE: Someone was saying, them 'turbans' make so much power they'll have extra left over. To sell to England!

EAMON: What? A millon euro to destroy our hill with those yokes, so they can sell power to the Brits! And you and me can't cut a bag of turf below for our own fires. There's something wrong somewhere, Nashee!

NASHEE: There is Eamon. You're right. Something wrong somewhere.

EAMON: Martin will be turning in his grave, Lord have mercy… and he hardly in it.

NASHEE: Well, I'm not sure if he will. I think Martin started the ball rolling with that crowd before he died. He had 'em in surveying and doing all kinds of measurements.

EAMON: I bet ya he did! Typical feckin' Martin! Throwing in the towel. A great man when you're five points up, but if you're two down with a minute to go, he goes missing!

NASHEE: Well, he's gone missing now anyway. (*A beat as they stare at the bag of turf.*)

EAMON: Feckin' quitter that's what he was. (*EAMON wallops it with the hurl.*)

NASHEE: Ah, Eamon, don't smash up his bit of turf. Sure the poor man was entitled to make arrangements for his future.

EAMON: Oh! What arrangements have you made?

SOUND: *Crows cawing.*

NASHEE: Well sure I… I'm… maybe Martin felt twas time to take it easy. He wasn't going to stay going up and down that hill for too many more winters, was he? He wasn't even looking forward to Christmas. On his own on Christmas day last year he was. All day.

EAMON: So was I!

NASHEE: Why didn't you call down to him?

EAMON: Because.

NASHEE: Ye were going through one of yeer 'not talking' phases. I'm not blaming you! I'm saying maybe he decided he'd had enough hardship.

EAMON: And the minute he decided to stop he keeled over, didn't he? That's what happens. Fellas stop what they've been doing all their lives, and take the soft option, and the next thing, bang! They're gone. Out the gap! You won't see me going down that road.

NASHEE: Well, what are you going to do?

EAMON: I'm going to get fit again, Nashee, that's what. When this hip is better, I'm going to join that Body Sculpt place in the town.

NASHEE: The gymnasium!

EAMON: Yeah.

NASHEE: Are you gone mad altogether?

EAMON: Why wouldn't I? I heard this doctor in the hospital telling a fella beside me about all these fitness programmes. And this fella was ten stone heavier than I am!

NASHEE: And probably twenty years younger.

EAMON: What are you trying to say?

NASHEE: Well, we're not going to live forever, are we?

EAMON: Why aren't we? Who made that rule? How do you know but I might be the first man to live forever.

NASHEE: Jaysus!

EAMON: I might! You know why? Because I'm not going to give in. That's why. Attitude, Nashee. That's the mistake people make. They give up! And they bring it on themselves. 'I think it; therefore I am it.' Plato said that!

NASHEE: Who?

EAMON: Plato. The philosopher. And he knew his stuff. Well, I have no intention of dying. Ye can all keep yeer dying. I'll be cutting turf next summer, and the summer after that, and the summer after that again, and woe betide whoever tries to stop me.

NASHEE: Ah, for God's sake!

EAMON: Where are you going?

NASHEE: I'm going down to put on a few spuds for me dinner.

EAMON: Hold on a minute! I haven't seen anyone right for weeks. I have something I want to ask you. Hold on and talk to me.

NASHEE: Listen to you, you mean.

EAMON: What?

NASHEE: You don't let me get a word in. There's no talking to you when you're in this humour.

EAMON: What do you want to talk about?

NASHEE: Nothing! I just want to go down and put on me dinner.

EAMON: What are you having?

NASHEE: You'll never guess.

EAMON: What?

NASHEE: Bacon and cabbage. Bit of white stuff on the side.

EAMON: Go way outa that, ya pillock.

NASHEE: You'll come down for a bit?

EAMON: Ah, I won't bother.

NASHEE: Arra do. Maybe we'd manage a drop, seeing as you're home.

EAMON: Sure, I might so. I never got a chance to get the few messages, the ambulance wouldn't stop at the LIDL coming home. That reminds me, I need you after the dinner.

NASHEE: For what?

EAMON: I want you to give me a leg up on the Massey.

NASHEE: You can't drive the three five in your state.

EAMON: I can so! All I need is a leg up.

NASHEE: You're not driving into the LIDL, are you?

EAMON: Why not? Anyway, I want to get a right look at the land since I was away.

NASHEE: The land is no different, I assure you. And how will you get down off it?

EAMON: I'll jump off that bridge when I come to it.

NASHEE: Well, we'll worry about the tractor later. Come on away down and we'll have the bit of dinner.

EAMON: Alright

EAMON: Hey, what's that in your yard?

NASHEE: What?

EAMON: I saw it earlier from above, but the henhouse was in the way. (*EAMON looks through the binoculars.*) Is it a skip?

NASHEE: Tis yeah.

EAMON: What are you doing with a skip?

NASHEE: Sure we're not allowed burn anything now.

EAMON: What would you be burning?

NASHEE: Ah, I did a bit of a cleanout. Don't be bothering looking. Tis only auld junk that was gathering dust.

EAMON focuses the binoculars as he looks down at the skip.

EAMON: That's the feckin' couch! From your kitchen. You threw out the couch!

NASHEE: Sure I have me chair by the fire.

EAMON: And is that the old wireless sticking out, the Marconi!

NASHEE: Yeah.

EAMON: Sure that's an antique, Nashee. That's worth money!

NASHEE: It got broke.

EAMON: How'd it get broke?

NASHEE: I don't know. How does anything get broke? Anyway, Father Meara gave me a grand little transistor instead.

EAMON: I bet ya he did.

NASHEE: Here will you stop gawping down into me skip.

EAMON: And that's the Child Of Prague statue, is it. Eileen's statue! That she got in Lourdes, God be good to her.

NASHEE: How can you see all that from here?

EAMON: Sure these yokes can focus in from a mile away. What's the Child Of Prague doing in the skip?

NASHEE: That got broke aswell. The head is gone off it.

EAMON: Jasus Christ! Did you break everything in the feckin' house?

NASHEE: No! I gave a few bits to Nuala and Father Meara. Things were only gathering dust. What?

EAMON: Nothing.

SOUND: Sound of the engine of a van in the distance.

EAMON: Tis just, I can't understand why you'd...

NASHEE: Shush! Whist!

EAMON: What?

NASHEE: Whist! D'ya hear that?

EAMON: What?

NASHEE: Whist, will you!

EAMON: Don't you be whisting me!

NASHEE: That's a van. Come back behind the gate, will you!

EAMON: Sure, Jasus, I can look down the feckin' hill, can't I?

NASHEE: Do you see anything?

EAMON: No.

NASHEE: I thought you could see everything with those.

EAMON: It doesn't see round feckin' turns, does it?

SOUND: The engine sound fading.

EAMON: Gone now whoever it was. Ya alright?

NASHEE: I'm grand.

EAMON: You hardly ever see a car back this way now, or even up at the road since the bypass. One time if you saw the lights of a car hitting the cowhouse at night you'd be reaching for the kettle – expecting a bit of news or something. Now, you see lights at night, you're reaching for the gun.

NASHEE: Are you not afraid?

EAMON: Of what?

NASHEE: That they'll come back.

EAMON: Sure what can I do? Only soldier on.

NASHEE: Twas very quiet around here with the both of ye gone.

EAMON: I suppose it was. What did you do with yourself at all?

NASHEE: Well sure, when I got tired looking out, I went out and looked in! (*They share a good laugh. A beat.*) All joking aside though; only for Father Meara dropping me to the churchyard to change Eileen's flowers and calling down the few times with the messages, I'da seen nare a soul at all. Me own niece hardly called down even!

EAMON: Father Meara! He'd rob ya without the ballyclava!

NASHEE: A good Christian man is what he is!

EAMON: He is, and his legs under every half right table in the town.

NASHEE: Well, if tis a thing I don't live forever, I'll be leaving him a few pound.

EAMON: For what?

NASHEE: For the church roof. The restoration fund.

EAMON: Well, that beats all! How long have they been restoring that roof now?

NASHEE: I don't know.

EAMON: Twenty-five years! Twenty-five years they've been codding the few shillings we have out of us, for a roof that's no different now than when they started this… feckin' scam!

NASHEE: It's not a scam.

EAMON: Is it not? There's not a whole lot wrong with his own roof you'll notice. And a carpet above under him in his sitting room you could sink to the axle in. And a fine car parked on his new gravel.

NASHEE: What exactly are you saying?

EAMON: I'm saying you'd want to cop on to yourself, Nashee!

NASHEE: The whole world is wrong with you today.

EAMON: The whole world is wrong this long time, and you throwing your few pound to Father Meara isn't going to fix it. The minute me back is turned, the vultures are in. You're being taken advantage of, Nashee. That's all I'm saying.

NASHEE: Well, that's something at least.

EAMON: What is?

NASHEE: That you're finished talking about it.

EAMON: Huh huh! I'll say no more. (*EAMON takes a few steps away with difficulty. He arches his back. It's clear he's in pain. The hurley slips and he stumbles.*)

NASHEE: A crutch'd be better than that hurl.

EAMON: The walk down took it out of me. Don't remember the lane being so steep. I'll sit a minute and get me breath. (*EAMON sits on the tree stump with difficulty. He takes out a cigarette and goes to light it.*)

NASHEE: You're not going to get your breath smoking!

EAMON: Jasus, you're worse than the doctors! Did I tell you they thought twas a miracle I found the strength to phone the ambulance for meself?

NASHEE: No.

EAMON: Do you have a match?

NASHEE: I have not! And if I had, I wouldn't give it to you.

EAMON: Tis a wonder you saw nor heard nothing that night.

NASHEE: What are you trying to say?

EAMON: What? Nothing. Only, you'd usually hear a van on the lane.

NASHEE: Yeah? I must have gone to bed early that night. What are you looking at me like that for?

EAMON: I'm only looking at you is all. What the hell is wrong with you?

NASHEE: There's nothing wrong with me. What did you want to ask me?

EAMON: What?

NASHEE: Earlier on, you wanted to ask me something.

EAMON: I was only wondering will you be going to Nuala's again? For Christmas.

NASHEE: Oh!

EAMON: Cause, if twas a thing you didn't feel like going to her, I'd say it can be fairly lively there with the kids.

NASHEE: Sure they're all grown up.

EAMON: Are they? Anyway, I was going to say... you could come up to me, if you wanted, or I could go down to you, if it suits, that is? What?

NASHEE: I don't rightly know about Christmas yet, or what I'll be doing, but if I'm around, sure of course I'll come up to you. And thanks for asking me.

EAMON: Why wouldn't you be around?

NASHEE: No why. Will we go down so? Or do you want to sit there a bit longer?

EAMON: I do in me arse. Here, take the end of the hurl and pull me up. (*NASHEE takes the unlit cigarette from him, throws it away and hauls EAMON up.*) Ohh! Lord God!

NASHEE: Y'alright? Here let me…

EAMON: Don't mind holding me! Jasus! I'm not a child!

NASHEE: Sorry.

EAMON: I just need to get going again. (*NASHEE watches as EAMON hobbles about. He does some pathetic attempts at hand to knee exercises, hips apart.*) Ohhh, I'll tell you one thing, Nashee. The feckin' bed takes it out of ya. I say, the bed takes it out of ya.

NASHEE: Are you trying to do a bit too much too soon maybe?

EAMON: Not at all. Another few days I'll be jogging!

SOUND: An engine, distant but gradually growing closer.

NASHEE: Well, maybe you should… shush, whist.

EAMON: What.

NASHEE: That's that van again. Do you hear it?

EAMON: No.

NASHEE: Listen. (*EAMON looks through the binoculars.*) Well, what can you see?

EAMON: I can't see anything at all.

NASHEE: Here give me a look. (*NASHEE grabs the binoculars from EAMON.*)

EAMON: Ow. Ow. Ow! Jasus! The strap is around me neck, ya feckin' gom ya. Are you trying to strangle me or what?

NASHEE: Sorry. I just need to see is all.

EAMON: Will you relax and let me look. (*EAMON focuses the binoculars.*)

SOUND: Engine nearing.

EAMON: Tis a van alright.

NASHEE: Where? Where is it?

EAMON: Coming along the lane. (*EAMON watches the progress of the van.*)

NASHEE: What's it doing? What's it doing, Eamon?

EAMON: Tis… tis… tis… moving along.

NASHEE: Moving along where?

EAMON: Tis coming towards…

NASHEE: Towards where?

EAMON: Towards your gate.

NASHEE: What colour is it? Hey! What colour is it?

EAMON: Tis a sort of a dark colour. Black, I'd say.

NASHEE: Jasus Christ. Here, come back behind here and don't let them see ya, Eamon. Will you come back here, will ya! Eamon!

EAMON: They're after turning into your yard.

SOUND: The distant engine running.

EAMON: They're stopped. Jasus.

NASHEE: What? What's happening?

EAMON: There's two of them after getting out.

NASHEE: What are they doing?

EAMON: They're… they're trying your back door. They're knocking at it, it looks like. They're looking in your window now!

NASHEE: Christ almighty, Eamon! Will you come back here, will you please? Eamon!

EAMON: They're at your skip. They looking in the skip. I'd say they're scrap fellas going the road.

NASHEE: Ah God! This is awful. Will you please come back here, Eamon?

EAMON: They're taking something.

NASHEE: What? What are they taking?

EAMON: I can't rightly see. It's… The Marconi. The wireless. They're after taking the Marconi.

SOUND: Two van doors opening and closing. The van drives away and fades into the distance.

EAMON: I told you twas valuable. Jasus Christ, Nashee! They're driving away. Do you think we should phone the guards.

NASHEE: No! We will not.

EAMON: Sure we have to. That wireless is worth money, even if it is broken. The guards might be able to catch…

NASHEE: I said no! We're not phoning any guards!

EAMON: What's wrong with you?

NASHEE: Just leave me alone for a minute!

EAMON watches him as he sits on the stile. A beat.

EAMON: Are you okay, Nashee?

NASHEE: I'm not able for any more of this, Eamon.

EAMON: Any more of what?

NASHEE: Just… leave it, Eamon.

EAMON: Alright.

SOUND: Crows Cawing.

(*A beat.*) Bit of a nip in that breeze now.

NASHEE: Yeah.

EAMON: Do you mind me asking you something?

NASHEE: Yeah. I do.

EAMON: Why were you carrying the billhook in the first place? It's not like it's a lot of use to you this time of year.

NASHEE: I don't know.

EAMON: Nashee...

NASHEE: What?

EAMON: Just.

NASHEE: If you have something to say, say it.

EAMON: Well, I don't think you came up here to fix the stile. I saw you out me window. You stopped and looked up at my place, and then turned back for home, and then turned back again. Twas only when I stirred out, you started poking at the stile.

NASHEE: So, what are you saying?

EAMON: I don't know! *(A beat.)* A bit of a clean out, you said – that you did below.

NASHEE: So? What?

EAMON: Well now, Nashee, whatever about getting rid of the couch, or even the Marconi, which was worth a bit, there's no way in the wide earthly world that you would have thrown out your Eileen's Child Of Prague that she spent all her life praying to, God be good to her. So... there's something up. Nashee? Are you going to tell me what it is? You're shaking. Are you alright?

NASHEE: They broke it.

EAMON: What?

NASHEE: They smashed up our little statue, same as they did everything else in the house.

EAMON: Who did?

NASHEE: Them dirty robbing blackguards. Who do you think? The night they robbed you, Eamon; they robbed me too. Broke everything in the place, set fire to the couch, I managed to quench it after, but I had to throw it out. Terrified I was. Terrified out of me wits. But they got nothing only what was in me pockets, cause I had nothing to give.

EAMON: Why didn't you tell the guards?

NASHEE: They said if I breathed a word they'd come back. I pretended I was blind so's they wouldn't beat me. Curled up in the corner so I did, and told them to take all they wanted.

EAMON: The thieving, cowardly, bastards. I'm awful sorry that happened ya, Nashee. Here, you've no need to worry now. Straighten yourself up. Dry your eyes there. We'll be grand.

NASHEE: That's why Father Meara got me to go to the team of fifty-nine reunion. He told Martin to bring me, he said twould do me good to get out and see a few people.

EAMON: So you told Martin?

NASHEE: Yeah.

EAMON: And Father Meara? And Martin never said a word to me when he came to see me.

NASHEE: I asked him not to.

EAMON: Why? (*NASHEE can't answer.*)

SOUND: Wild geese honking across the sky.

EAMON: More geese heading in.

NASHEE: Here. (*Handing him a tightly folded envelope.*)

EAMON: What's that?

NASHEE: There's five hundred euro there. For you.

EAMON: For me? Why?

NASHEE: I told them where you kept the turf money. Sorry, Eamon. They asked me about you. Said they heard you were a bit of a tough nut. We'll see how tough he is, one of 'em said. I knew you'd never tell 'em where the money was, so, I said, if they promised not to harm you…

EAMON: You told them where it was.

NASHEE: Yeah. And they beat you up anyway.

EAMON: Well, I didn't make it easy for 'em, put it that way.

NASHEE: Not like me! There's days I wish they'd beaten me too and that's the truth. They ripped me phone out of the wall, I couldn't even warn ya.

EAMON: My God, Nashee. Tis a sad state we're in, at the end of our days.

NASHEE: I'm awful sorry, Eamon…

EAMON: There's no need for you to be sorry! Here! Put that back in your pocket. We'll say no more about it. Take it, I'm telling you! You did what you felt you had to do. You were backed into a corner. Who's to say I wouldn't have done the same meself?

NASHEE: As if you would! You're a sound man, Eamon. Sound out. I won't forget it to you.

EAMON: Do you know what we are, Nashee?

NASHEE: No. What?

EAMON: We're exiles in our own Godforsaken land.

NASHEE: Yeah. I suppose we are.

SOUND: *Crows cawing.*

EAMON: Come on.

NASHEE: Where are you going?

EAMON: I'm going to get a few nails to finish fixing this, Nashee. And you're going to help me. We'll not be beaten by 'em! By Christ we won't! (*He sees NASHEE's letter and can't resist taking it out of his pocket.*)

NASHEE: Hey! That's me letter! You took it outa me coat. Give us it.

EAMON: (*Reading*) Mr Ignatius Finn… recent application… The nursing home. The home! You're going into the home!

NASHEE: I am.

EAMON: When are you going?

NASHEE: A fortnight. That's the official confirmation. The matron told Nuala last week. I'll be in for Christmas.

EAMON: That was the post van this morning? When were you going to tell me?

NASHEE: Sure I was trying to! I was working up to it. I didn't know how I was going to tell you.

EAMON: You don't have to go! There's not a thing wrong with you, Nashee – if you got the proper glasses you'd be right as rain!

NASHEE: I've had enough, Eamon.

EAMON: Look! You've had a bit of a shock, fair enough, but… them fellas below there today, they were only a couple of scrap fellas going the road. Sure once you put a skip out the whole country comes calling. They were probably knocking on your door to ask you was it okay to take the stuff.

NASHEE: No

EAMON: Nashee, you can't just up and leave, I mean… You can't do that! You can't.

NASHEE: I'm tired, Eamon.

EAMON: Sure we're all tired! Look it, we'll get the winter over us. You'll feel different then.

NASHEE: I won't! I'm afraid, Eamon. I'm afraid. Terrified, every single night, in me own house. Walking around in the day with a billhook! No more than yourself with the binoculars. To see 'em coming. Isn't that the reason you bought 'em? Isn't it? I don't blame you. Well, now I want a bit of comfort. And a bit of peace. I'm entitled to it. And I'm going to have it. I'm going to take the bed in the home. Me mind is made up.

EAMON: I'll pay you.

NASHEE: What?

EAMON: To stay. I'll pay you to stay. Whatever amount you want!

NASHEE: Sure tis not money I want, Eamon. You know that.

EAMON: Where does that leave me? I mean… What am I going to do now?

NASHEE: I don't know, Eamon.

EAMON: There's no changing your mind, no?

NASHEE: No, Eamon.

EAMON: Ahh Lord. Tis not right. Exiles, Nashee, that's what we are.

NASHEE: Will we go down and have the bit of bacon?

EAMON: Do you know, I don't think I will.

NASHEE: Ah come on down with me.

EAMON: I won't bother, Nashee. The walk back up might be a bit much for one day. I'll come down another day before you… before you go. Maybe tomorrow?

NASHEE: I won't be here tomorrow. Nuala is taking me to town to get pyjamas and a few things for… you know.

EAMON: Oh. Right.

NASHEE: Do you still want a leg up on the Massey later on?

EAMON: No. Be dark soon now anyway.

NASHEE: You could stay down at my place, till you got the place tidied up above, if you wanted. Until I go, like.

EAMON: I'll manage by myself, Nashee. Thanks anyway.

NASHEE: Right. Right. I might head away down so, before it gets dark.

EAMON: Go on then.

NASHEE: Right.

EAMON: (*As NASHEE departs…*) You'll hardly be needing me billhook in the home!

NASHEE: Oh! No. Don't suppose I will. Here.

As NASHEE hands him back the billhook, neither can let it go. There's a lifetime of unspoken friendship in this grip.

SOUND: Crows cawing.

They finally manage a nod to each other. NASHEE lets go of the billhook. He's unable to leave.

EAMON: You know, the crows never nested as low beyond in the ringfort as they did his year. A bad sign.

NASHEE: Sure maybe I'll see you some day before I go.

EAMON: You will. You will. Of course you will. Sure don't we have to fix the gate?

NASHEE: Yeah.

EAMON: Yeah. Good luck, Nashee.

NASHEE: Good luck, Eamon. There's a hard frost coming I'd say. (*NASHEE goes.*)

EAMON: Yeah. A right hard frost.

SOUND: Whistle section at the end of the song 'The Quiet Land Of Erin'.

EAMON stands alone with his billhook and hurl. The lights fade to black.

THE END

Cirque des Rêves
Katie McCann

First produced in Bewley's Café Theatre in October 2016.

DIRECTOR: Jeda de Brí
SET DESIGN: Aoife Fealy
ADDITIONAL SET DESIGN: Sinéad Purcell
LIGHTING DESIGN: Maggie Donovan
COSTUME DESIGN: Nicola Burke
COMPOSER: Eoghan O'Shaughnessy
MUSICAL ARRANGEMENT: Agnese Banti
MUSICAL ARRANGEMENT / VOCAL COACHING: Silvia Lombardi François
VISUAL DESIGN: Ste Murray

CHARACTERS & CAST:
POPPY PARKER: Clodagh Mooney Duggan
MR SPARROW / FIRST MATE / FATHER / MR KILLJAY / STEVE GRIMALDI / RINGMASTER / NARRATOR 2: Finbarr Doyle
GIRL / CECILY / LIVING DOLL / ASSISTANT / FORTUNE TELLER / NARRATOR 3: Katie McCann
MR NIGHTINGALE / PIRATE / TRISTAN / ENTERTAINER / DAVE GRIMALDI / MR SCARAMANTUS / NARRATOR 1: Kevin Olohan

---

Katie McCann is a Dublin-based actor, writer and producer. She trained at the Gaiety School of Acting and has a BA in English from UCD. Her other stage plays include *The Little Match Girl, Tales from Briar Hall, Hollow Ground* and *The Grimm Tale of Cinderella*. For television, Katie has worked with Tailored Films and RTÉ. She is the Artistic Director of Illustrated Productions.

The action of the play takes place between two realities. The first is Whitechapel, London, in 1886; the second is that of the story of the young Poppy Parker. Switches between worlds are marked with the following: ***********

A slash (/) indicates where one character begins speaking over another.

A cold night inside an abandoned warehouse in Whitechapel, London, in 1886. Two men sit drinking in the darkness. A girl enters. She is carrying a battered old suitcase and a stick with a scarf tied to the end. She is being watched by the two men. They have spotted their latest mark.

MR SPARROW: Awful late to be wandering around on your todd, my dear.

MR NIGHTINGALE: This ain't the type of neighbourhood to be taking a midnight stroll in, my little poppet.

MR SPARROW: Lucky she ran into us and not any… unsavoury characters. Specially at such an hour as this.

MR NIGHTINGALE: Oh yes, lots of unsavoury characters round these parts. Very lucky indeed. Don't you worry, my dear, you're in safe hands with us, ain't she?

MR SPARROW: Oh the best. The very best.

MR NIGHTINGALE: So what's a sweet little thing like you doing round here all on your own?

The girl stares at them, very wary and defiant, but says nothing.

MR SPARROW: Maybe she's lost? (*Shouting at her like she's deaf.*) Lost, are you?

MR NIGHTINGALE: Certainly what it looks like…

MR SPARROW: (*He attempts to pickpocket her as he speaks.*) Or perhaps she's looking for someone? (*Shouting again.*) You looking for someone, girlie?

GIRL: None of your business!

MR SPARROW: Cheeky, ain't she?

MR NIGHTINGALE: A bit too smart for her own good I'd say. Ain't you ever heard that little girls are suppose to be seen and not heard?

MR SPARROW: Children these days, Mr Nightingale, ain't got no idea about how to behave in civilised company.

MR NIGHTINGALE: Oh, Mr Sparrow, never a truer word spoken. Ain't you afraid, poppet, being out this late, all on your own? Don't you know there's a ripper on the loose?

MR SPARROW: If you're not careful he might slice you up and gut you like a fish.

GIRL: No, he won't.

MR NIGHTINGALE: What makes you so sure, eh? You might be just his type?

GIRL: My dad says he only slices up ladies of ill repute. Them that drinks in the Ten Bells and sells more than their apples and pears. That's what my dad said.

MR SPARROW: Ain't your dad a clever one. I bet you take right after him, don't you?

MR NIGHTINGALE: Then tell me this and tell me no more… what's a nice young lady like you doing out here on her own? You should be tucked up all nice and neat in your bed. I mean ain't you scared? Ripper or no ripper, this ain't no place for a little girl.

GIRL: I'm not a little girl and I ain't afraid. Besides I can take care of myself.

MR SPARROW: If you ain't looking for someone, and you ain't lost, then what are you doing prowling the streets so late at night?

GIRL: I ain't doing nothing.

MR NIGHTINGALE: Don't look like nothing. Looks like snooping.

MR SPARROW: Maybe she's a member of one of them gangs. I hear all the little kiddies are in gangs these days.

MR NIGHTINGALE: Well she certainly ain't up to any good, that much is sure. She's probably scouting the place out for potential victims.

MR SPARROW: I think we might have to notify the necessary authorities.

GIRL: No don't!

MR NIGHTINGALE: These are dangerous times, my girl. Can't be taking any risks. Once you spot someone sneaking around, all suspicious like, you gotta act before it's too late.

MR SPARROW: Yeah. Got to think of the integrity of the whole neighbourhood. Property prices and that.

MR NIGHTINGALE: After all, for all we know, you could be the Ripper…

GIRL: What? Don't/ be silly.

MR SPARROW: /Oh, yeah, she does have the cold dead eyes of a killer alright./

GIRL: No, I ain't/…

MR NIGHTINGALE: /That's just what the Ripper would say, isn't it? Here, Mr Sparrow, go fetch the bobby we saw back on Fournier Street. He's probably still finishing off his pint.

GIRL: No! Don't, please! I ain't done nothing.

MR SPARROW: Guilty until proven innocent, my friend. You won't talk to us but they'll soon have you talking down the clink. Oh they'll have you squealing like a little piggy.

GIRL: But I was just/…

MR NIGHTINGALE: /Just what?

GIRL: I was… running away, if you must know. That's all. Don't call no one. I swear I ain't done anything.

MR SPARROW: Running away from home, my, my. What you running from?

GIRL: Nothing.

MR SPARROW: Everyone's running from something.

GIRL: (*She looks at them intently.*) Not that it's any of your business but if you must know I'm running away to join the circus.

Pause… then they burst out laughing.

MR SPARROW: Why on earth would you wanna run away with the circus?

GIRL: (*Her pride is hurt.*) Because it's exciting. More exciting than school and that. See! (*She takes out her flyer to show them.*)

MR NIGHTINGALE: (*Takes it, glances at it then throws it away.*) Very nice, I'm sure. But ain't you scared?

GIRL: I told you I ain't scared of nothing.

MR NIGHTINGALE: Oh, but you should be. You see running away from home is one thing. Not a bad idea in my opinion. Lots of fine people have run away from home, but running away with the circus… well that's something else altogether.

GIRL: What you mean?

MR NIGHTINGALE: Ain't you ever heard of Poppy Parker?

GIRL: Who?

MR SPARROW: Who? (*MR NIGHTINGALE hits him.*) Oh… oh right, yeah, poor old Poppy Parker… dreadful business that.

MR NIGHTINGALE: An awful affair altogether.

Cirque des Rêves

GIRL: Why? What happened to her?

MR NIGHTINGALE: Well… she got all mixed up with a circus too, you see. But things… They didn't really work out as she had hoped.

GIRL: What you mean?

MR NIGHTINGALE: You see you got to be careful with them artistic folks. Things are never what they seem with them. Bunch of liars and thieves, every last one of them. She learned that all too well, just a little too late.

GIRL: They do something to her?

MR SPARROW: Oh it's a very sad story, very sad indeed, you wouldn't really want to hear it, believe me. And considering your intended trajectory for the evening… well, it might make you see things a little differently.

GIRL: Tell me.

MR SPARROW: I dunno… it's not really a story for little girls. Might give you nightmares and that. Plus I would hate to think that we could influence your decision, intentionally or unintentionally.

GIRL: I won't get nightmares, I swear. Please tell me the story!

MR SPARROW: All right but don't say we didn't warn you because this isn't a story for the faint of heart. No. This is the type of story that can turn the hair on your head pure white and chill the marrow inside your very/ bones…

GIRL: /Are you gonna tell me the story or are you just gonna keep talking about telling me the story?

MR SPARROW: Alright, keep your hat on. I was just creating a sense of ominous foreboding but I can see it's lost on you. Right… how does it begin, Mr Nightingale?

MR NIGHTINGALE: Like any good story, Mr Sparrow… Not so very long ago, in a place not so very far from here, there lived a girl by the name of Poppy Parker.

****

Enter POPPY PARKER.

POPPY: Poppy Petunia Primrose Parker.

NARRATOR 1: Was the daughter of a world-renowned botanist and Professor of rare and exotic flora and fauna.

NARRATOR 2: The apple of her parent's eye, she was what many would describe as an excellent example of a perfectly pleasant young woman.

NARRATOR 1: Polite, accommodating and with a healthy appetite for the outdoors, Poppy had all the makings of becoming a very accomplished young lady.

NARRATOR 3: Unfortunately her one shortcoming was that she possessed what could, well, only be described as/

POPPY slips into a daydream that comes to life.

FIRST MATE: /Captain Parker!

NARRATOR 3: An over-active imagination.

FIRST MATE: One-eyed Pete says he's spotted a ship, Captain, hot on our tail. Gaining fast, he says. She's flying the Jolly Rodger. Looks likely to be the Cuttle Throat, Captain.

POPPY: Batten down the hatches and hoist the sails. Clear the deck and tell the men to hold fast to the course.

FIRST MATE: We cannot outrun her, Captain. They say that the Cuttle Throat never leaves a man alive. We're doomed, Captain. Doomed I say!

POPPY: Do not loose heart, Mr Harker. If we cannot outrun her, we shall have to meet her head on.

FIRST MATE: But Captain!

POPPY: To your post, Mr Harker. We hold our ground.

PIRATE: Well, well, well. If it isn't little Miss Poppy Parker.

PARROT: (*Squawk.*) Poppy Parker!

POPPY: Captain Thorn. A pleasure as always.

PIRATE: We've come for your treasure, girlie. Hand her over and I may let you live.

PARROT: (*Squawk.*) May let you live! (*Whistle.*)

POPPY: It's Captain Parker to you, and you can have it over my dead body.

PIRATE: That can quickly be arranged.

POPPY: Take your crew and leave, Thorn. These are good men and I will not allow you to harm them.

PIRATE: (*Laughs along with Parrot.*) And who be you to stop me? Come, come, let us put our differences aside. Join with me, girlie, and you could become a part of one of the most feared crew on the seven seas. Together there'll be no ship to match us.

POPPY: And set aside my honour to become a pirate like you? Thank you for your kind offer but I am afraid that I must decline.

PARROT: (*Squawk.*) Sassy!

PIRATE: Then on your head be it.

POPPY: Have at thee, scoundrel!

They go to fight but before they reach each other POPPY is snapped back to reality by her teacher, MR KILLJAY.

MR KILLJAY: Poppy Parker! If you would be so kind as to re-join us here in the land of the living!

POPPY: Sorry, Mr Killjay, won't happen again, sir.

MR KILLJAY: Well, now that we have you back in the room, if you would kindly repeat after me…

NARRATOR 3: You see everyday life was not something that Poppy felt any sort of connection with.

MR KILLJAY: *Et magna decore his, putant tibique democritum…*

POPPY goes back to looking incredibly bored.

NARRATOR 3: Poppy would spend hours and hours daydreaming about the life she could be living as opposed to engaging in the life she actually was. And because of this she was continually being scolded and reprimanded by her teachers, much to the annoyance of her father.

NARRATOR 1: Mr Parker was not the type of man to engage in childish fantasy or what was commonly referred to as 'whimsy'. He had been top of his class, even in preschool.

NARRATOR 3: He had never failed an exam, never misbehaved in school and, in fact, he had never done anything interesting in his entire life.

FATHER: Poppy, dear, this cannot be allowed to continue. You have to stop walking around with your head in the clouds like some dimwit and focus on your education. Knowledge is power, you know.

POPPY: But what's the point in learning all these things from books when instead I could be going out into the world and really seeing them. Surely there is more value in that?

FATHER: I hardly think that would be appropriate for a young girl of your situation. You're not some sort of street urchin crawling around a Dickens novel.

POPPY: But I want to do things, go places, discover the world for myself. Why can't I go on great adventures and see the pyramids, and the Colosseum, and the temples of Peru? It's not fair!

FATHER: For God sake, Poppy, life is not fair! You're not a child anymore and I will no longer amuse these childish fantasies of yours. It's time you grew up and got your head out of the clouds. This is the real world and it's time you started living in it. *(He leaves.)*

POPPY: But, father!

CECILY: Morning, Poppy.

POPPY: Morning, Cecily.

CECILY: What's wrong? You don't seem like your usual overly enthusiastic self?

POPPY: It's nothing really...

CECILY: Oh, well, good because I have news.

POPPY: Really? Has something happened?

CECILY: Yes, Mrs Lockley got a delivery of three new types of ribbon from London yesterday and Mama says that if I'm good /she might take me...

POPPY: /Oh for goodness sake!

CECILY: Poppy! Language, please.

POPPY: I'm sorry but... how can you stand it?

CECILY: Stand what?

POPPY: Everything. It's just so... boring. Everyday, it's the same thing over and over again. Don't you wish there was... more?

CECILY: Oh, Poppy, what a silly thing to say. I mean, what more is there?

POPPY: Yes... I suppose so.

TRISTAN: Morning, Poppy.

POPPY: Good morning, Tristan.

TRISTAN: Have you heard?

POPPY: Oh yes, I've heard all about the new ribbons!

TRISTAN: What? No! Over at Potter's field? They just pitched up last night. Father says it was like a well-organised invasion, under the cover of darkness, very sneaky, that's what he said. It's just like when the foxes built their den under our shed./

POPPY: /Tristan...

TRISTAN:/They just appeared out of nowhere /

POPPY: /Tristan…

TRISTAN: and by the time we realised they were there, there was no getting rid of them./

POPPY: /Tristan…

TRISTAN: They do awful things to mother's azaleas/

POPPY: /Tristan! What are you talking about?

TRISTAN: Oh, sorry, yes… The circus. Well, a circus. Turned up last night. Haven't you seen them?

POPPY: A circus! Really?

TRISTAN: No one even knew they were coming. Not even Mrs Lockley and she knows everyone's business.

POPPY: How curious.

TRISTAN: Yeah. Father says it's just like those travelling types to arrive unannounced. Can't trust them as far as you can toss them.

POPPY: I think the circus is wonderful.

TRISTAN: Oh yeah, no, it is. Really… exciting and that. (*Pause.*) You… you wouldn't like to go and see it? Would you? I mean with me? Maybe… if you like. Or not. Only if you want / to. I don't mind. (*He trails off.*)

CECILY: /Poppy! Have you heard the news?

POPPY: Yes. Tristan was just telling me…

CECILY: Oh, Tristan it's you. Go away, will you.

TRISTAN: Oh right… yes…

CECILY: Now, Tristan.

TRISTAN: Of course… sorry to bother you. Bye, Poppy.

POPPY: Goodbye, Tristan.

CECILY: Mrs Lockley told Pam in the corner shop, who told Ms Tilly, who then told mother, who told me that the school are taking us to the circus!

POPPY: Really?

MR KILLJAY: Class! I believe you have heard the rumors and, yes, we shall indeed be attending the Circus at Potter's field. (*There is a rumbling of excitement from the class.*) Shut Up! The reason for this highly unorthodox excursion is that the headmaster feels it is important for you all to broaden your minds. That we must squash any xenophobic tendencies that you have been harbouring in your small yet under developed brains. Therefore this expedition is not to be viewed as any sort of recreational time but as an outing of cultural and sociological significance. One you will be tested on after.

Grumble of annoyance from TRISTAN and POPPY, squeal of excitement from CECILY.

NARRATOR 1: That evening Mr Killjay led the group of excited students towards the large field that lay on the edge of the town.

NARRATOR 2: On any other day Potter's field lay dormant, unused and abandoned. Most people too superstitious to venture past its walls.

NARRATOR 3: Once upon a time it had been the site for all the unconsecrated graves of the town.

NARRATOR 2: Witches and suicides had been laid to an uneasy rest there, outside of the churchyard walls with little more than the odd stone to mark the spot.

NARRATOR 1. But tonight superstition was forgotten, for as darkness began to fall and the full moon rose high in the clear night sky, Potters field was coming to life.

NARRATOR 3: Through the darkness there was an explosion of colour and sound unlike anything that had ever been seen there before.

NARRATOR 1: Fire eaters.

NARRATOR 3: Magicians.

NARRATOR 2: Juggling clowns.

NARRATOR 3: Poppy couldn't believe her eyes. This was everything she had ever wanted and so much more.

MR KILLJAY: Right, no one is to touch anything! You have no idea where these people have been and I will not be held responsible for you all catching some rare and disfiguring disease. I am speaking particularly to you, Voldersnout. I have my eye on you.

The movement of the children can be used to set up the stage for the performance. Moving props, etc. It should be chaotic and energetic.

CECILY: Poppy, look at this!

POPPY: Wait for me!

MR KILLJAY: Will you please desist from that infernal running about! You are not a Labrador, Voldersnout!

TRISTAN: Over here, Poppy!

POPPY: What is that?

MR KILLJAY: Come back here this instant! My God, it's like herding kittens!

TRISTAN: I want to see the elephants! No, the acrobats.

CECILY: Over here! Look over here!

RINGMASTER: Ladies and gentlemen, boys and girls, step right up to see the greatest show on earth! Le Cirque de Réves!

> SONG 1: RINGMASTER SONG #1
>
> Step forward that you might see
> The world as it could never be
> Feast your eyes unto their fill
> On such that strays 'tween good and ill.
>
> You may pass through highs and lows
> Shades and tones only the dreamer knows
> But hold your courage to your breast
> And we'll take care of all the rest.

> Wheels and cogs are spinning endlessly
> To keep this clockwork world in time
> Search the corners of your very mind
> And there the Living Doll you'll find.
>
> The stars are observing
> Clouds are obscuring
> The night is alluring
> Kindly behold the show!

As the RINGMASTER talks POPPY takes a seat in the audience to watch. THE GRIMALDI BROTHERS and their LIVING DOLL enter and perform their act. They fumble around as clowns do hitting each other over the head and tripping one another until they reveal the LIVING DOLL. She is stuck and lifeless. They seem to not know how to make her move. They try to start her up to no avail. They search for her key and wind her up. She comes to life singing a broken sad song.

LIVING DOLL: So long ago upon a d-d-d-dream,
A face a voice that haunts me still.
A love untold, a passion filled,
Lost upon… Lost upon… Lost upon…

THE LIVING DOLL begins to break as she reaches for POPPY longingly. As if she has something to say. Before she can touch POPPY, one of the GRIMALDI BROTHERS pulls the key, turning her out and she falls lifeless. End of act.

RINGMASTER: A round of applause for the Grimaldi brothers and their Living Doll! Thank you, ladies and gentlemen. We will now take a short break but we shall return with more extraordinary acts in a moment! Feel free to wander the tents. There are many strange, exciting things to uncover around every corner. But we would ask you to please not feed any of the animals. They are on a strict gluten-free diet and any tampering with this may result in their early demise. Thank you! (*He runs off after them as if slightly worried.*)

POPPY: Where have you been! You missed the first show!

CECILY: Come on, we're leaving.

POPPY: But they've only just started!

CECILY: I don't like it here, it's weird.

POPPY: It's not weird, it's different, that's all. Aren't you having fun?

CECILY: No, I am not having fun. This place is filthy and the people are filthy and none of it makes any sense and that confuses me and makes my brain hurt. So, no, I don't want to stay here any longer. I want to go home!

POPPY: Oh please, Cecily, stay just a little longer. It's the only fun thing that's ever happened in this town. Stay, please. For me?

CECILY: (*Reluctantly*) Oh, I suppose another half an hour couldn't hurt.

POPPY: Thank you.

TRISTAN: (*TRISTAN runs on, he is on a massive sugar high.*) Poppy have you seen the acrobats! They're amazing! (*As he jumps between them he accidentally knocks into CECILY.*)

CECILY: Oh for god sake, Tristan!

TRISTAN: Woops! Sorry about that!

CECILY: You are such a pest. Why are you even here, Tristan, no one wants you here, why don't you just… ugh! (*She storms off.*)

TRISTAN: It was an accident… Really it was. I didn't mean to upset her.

POPPY: I think she was upset already, you just didn't help matters.

TRISTAN: I can't seem to do anything right.

POPPY: Ignore her, she doesn't know what she's talking about. I like having you around.

TRISTAN: Really?

POPPY: Yes. Very much so.

TRISTAN: Wow. Great. Good to know. (*He stares at her for a moment awkwardly.*)

POPPY: Are you having a good time?

TRISTAN: *(Talking very quickly.)* Rather! They have hundreds of different types of sweets here. Cotton candy and cinnamon swirls and sweet popcorn. Mother doesn't usefully let me eat this much sugar. She says it makes me agitated. But I don't see what she's talking about. I've had six toffee apples already and I feel fine. Great! And quite hot. Are you hot? I do feel really rather / warm.

POPPY: /Tristan, maybe you should put the sweets away. Your mother might have been on to something.

TRISTAN: Right, yes. Maybe. Do you think I should go after Cecily and apologise?

POPPY: That's not a bad idea.

TRISTAN: Right back in a jiffy. *(Goes to leave then stops and turns back.)* Poppy, I couldn't… I mean… maybe… if you like… could I walk you home later? If you're going home that is. I mean, of course, you're going home, but if you are going at the same time as me? Maybe? Or not…

POPPY: That would be lovely, Tristan, thank you.

TRISTAN: Brilliant. Yes. That would be brilliant. Right. See you in a bit, I suppose…

He stands there awkwardly for a moment staring at her then runs away. POPPY is alone a moment, amused, looking for which tent to go exploring in when the FORTUNE TELLER appears. A blind, Eastern European lady covered in a dark veil.

FORTUNE TELLER: Hello, my dear…

POPPY: Oh! Hello. I'm sorry I didn't see you there.

FORTUNE TELLER: That makes two of us… *(She indicates she is blind.)*

POPPY: Oh dear, I didn't mean to… I didn't realise you were… ummmmm…

FORTUNE TELLER: Do not trouble yourself, child. After all there is more than one way to see the world.

POPPY: Father told me that when you lose one of your senses the others can become heightened.

FORTUNE TELLER: Oh, yes, indeed. Taste, touch, smell… among other things… Come here to me, my boy.

POPPY: I'm a girl.

FORTUNE TELLER: Hummmmm… interesting… Your aura. You have a spark of destiny about you.

POPPY: Well that's nice but I better be going.

FORTUNE TELLER: Of course. But before you go, would you like to have your fortune read?

POPPY: Excuse me?

FORTUNE TELLER: As I said there is more than one way to see the world. I just so happen to have the gift of the third eye. I can tell you what the fates have in store for you. That is if you wish to know?

POPPY: Oh well… yes, I suppose so.

FORTUNE TELLER: But first I must warn you, it can be dangerous dabbling in magic and the world beyond the veil holds many dangers. To know the future can cost you more than what is in your pocket, if you get my drift?

POPPY: Not really…

FORTUNE TELLER: Well, just cross my palm with silver and I shall look into the mists of time and reveal the secrets of the beyond.

POPPY looks at her confused. Pause.

FORTUNE TELLER: (*Dropping her accent for a moment.*) Give me some money.

POPPY: Oh right, yes.

FORTUNE TELLER: Give me your hand, boy. Ah! I see you hunger for adventure. That life has you trapped, trapped like a rat in a bucket of tuna. You long to see the world, to experience life to the full.

POPPY: Yes… but I already know all that.

FORTUNE TELLER: Give me a minute, I'm just warming up... I see that... yes! You will have adventures. Marvellous adventures! Adventures beyond your wildest dreams!

POPPY: Oh how wonderful! What else do you see?

FORTUNE TELLER: I see... a name... Do you know... a Steve or possibly a Stephen?

POPPY: No.

FORTUNE TELLER: Perhaps his brother Dave?

POPPY: Are you really a fortune teller?

FORTUNE TELLER: Of course I am. How dare you question me!

POPPY: You said I have a spark of destiny about me. Can't you be more specific?

FORTUNE TELLER: Fine. But it'll cost you extra. (*POPPY hands her another coin. FORTUNE TELLER takes out a deck of Tarot Cards, and produces first the wheel of fortune card.*) Yes, the wheel of fortune is turning for you good... (*Next: the moon card*) The moon! There is deception ahead, enemies hidden in every shadow. (*Lovers card*) Ah the lovers... you shall be tested... (*And finally she takes out the death card and jumps back afraid of what she's seen.*) Death... Oh no. Oh no, no, no...

POPPY: What does it mean?

FORTUNE TELLER: You must go. Leave this place.

POPPY: What?

FORTUNE TELLER: You are in grave danger, my young man.

POPPY: What do you mean? I thought you said I was going on an adventure.

FORTUNE TELLER: This is not the adventure you want. There is great darkness here and you must go before it finds you. Run, my boy! Run!

POPPY: But I don't understand!

ENTERTAINER: Oi watch it! Well… hello.

POPPY: I'm sorry I didn't mean to… I wasn't looking where I was going, forgive me.

ENTERTAINER: That's alright, my dear, consider it forgotten. Are you alright? You seem a bit agitated if you don't mind my saying.

POPPY: It's nothing. Just that lady she was saying some very strange things… about my destiny…

ENTERTAINER: Oh her? Crazy Meg? Wouldn't pay any notice to her. Off her rocker she is. Hope you didn't give her any money?

POPPY: I'm afraid I did.

ENTERTAINER: Pity, that'll be her down the rum shop for the day. Oh well, can't be helped. Now, perhaps I can help you?

POPPY: Well, I was going to watch the next performance but I think perhaps I best go home now.

ENTERTAINER: Nonsense! You can't let an old crazy like Loopy Lilly put you off.

POPPY: I thought you said her/ name was.

ENTERTAINER: /Doesn't matter. What I mean is you haven't come this far just to go home now, have you? Would be a waste.

POPPY: (*Considers this a moment.*) Yes, I suppose you're right.

ENTERTAINER: I know what you need. A change of pace. Perhaps I can interest you in The Hall of Dreams?

POPPY: What's that?

ENTERTAINER: Well if I told you, it would ruin the surprise, wouldn't it?

POPPY: The Hall of Dreams… alright, I suppose I can give it a go.

ENTERTAINER: That's the spirit! Right, if you just head down that way, keep going straight, to the back, it's the last tent on the left. Can't miss it…

POPPY: Thank you. (*She goes to leave.*)

ENTERTAINER: Even if your life depended on it.

She comes back.

POPPY: Sorry, what did you say?

ENTERTAINER: What? Oh, nothing just… mumbling suspiciously to myself that's all.

POPPY: Oh right. Thank you.

ENTERTAINER: You're very welcome, Miss Parker.

POPPY: Wait, how did you know my…?

NARRATOR 3: At the back of the field stood a single tent. A little away from the others, shabby, dark and alone.

NARRATOR 2: There was no sign of life or that anyone but Poppy had been there for a very long time.

NARRATOR 3: It was the type of place that most people would have turned away and run from.

NARRATOR 1: It was a place where most people would fear to enter.

NARRATOR 2: But Poppy Parker was not most people, and being the curious creature she was, she found herself unable to turn back.

POPPY: Hello? Is anyone here?

She steps forward and sees a mirror with a reflection in it played by another actor. They move in unison. The reflection copies her perfectly but it is not POPPY.

POPPY: How wonderful.

VOICE: Poppy…

She turns away from the mirror but the reflection doesn't follow – it stares at her then smiles and disappears.

POPPY: Hello? Who said that? Is someone there? (*POPPY turns back to the mirror to find the reflection gone.*) How did you…?

VOICE: Poppy…

POPPY: Tristan, is that you? (*She is growing uneasy.*) Tristan…

****

MR SPARROW: BOO!

We are thrown back into Whitechapel in 1886. The GIRL jumps and screams. Both MR SPARROW and MR NIGHTINGALE laugh uncontrollably.

GIRL: What did you do that for?

MR SPARROW: You should have seen your face! Priceless, it was.

GIRL: That's not funny.

MR SPARROW: It was pretty funny actually.

GIRL stands up and begins to walk away, her pride hurt, sulking.

MR NIGHTINGALE: Oh here don't be like that.

MR SPARROW: We'll behave, I promise! Come back!

GIRL: I didn't come here to be made fun of by you. I ain't no fool, and I ain't gonna be made into one, either. Goodnight, gentlemen.

MR NIGHTINGALE: Wait! If you leave now, you'll never know what happened. You'll spend your whole life wondering, 'What if I'd stayed? What would have happened? What sort of life affirming lesson would I have learned that could have steered my life in a better path had I just stayed and listened to the end of that charming man's story?'

GIRL: I don't trust you.

MR SPARROW: And well you shouldn't. (*He gets a dig off MR NIGHTINGALE.*) Ow!

MR NIGHTINGALE: What he means is: if you leave, you'll never know what happens next. And ain't you just a little bit curious?

GIRL: No.

MR NIGHTINGALE: I think you might be telling a bit of a porky pie there, my dear.

GIRL: (*She considers this a moment.*) If I come back, do you swear to behave yourselves?

MR NIGHTINGALE: Upon my soul!

MR SPARROW: Cross our hearts and hope to die.

MR NIGHTINGALE: We swear we will not do anything like that again while telling you this story.

Pause.

GIRL: Alright then.

GIRL comes back and joins them.

MR SPARROW: That's the spirit!

MR NIGHTINGALE: Alright… where were we? Oh yes…

****

We jump back into the story.

POPPY: Tristan? Tristan, is that you? Please, this isn't funny… Tristan…

RINGMASTER: May I be of assistance?

POPPY: Oh! I didn't see you there. Sorry for intruding.

RINGMASTER: Not at all. You are very welcome. I am Mousier De Winter, Ringmaster extraordinaire, how do you do…?

POPPY: Poppy, Poppy Parker.

RINGMASTER: What an exquisite name. Mademoiselle Parker. A pleasure.

POPPY: Likewise. (*Looking around.*) Is there a show on in here?

RINGMASTER: Not exactly. It is more of an exhibit than an exhibition. Remains of old acts. Please feel free to take a look around.

POPPY: (*She begins to wander around.*) I saw your show earlier. It was wonderful.

RINGMASTER: Thank you.

POPPY: How long are you staying?

RINGMASTER: We stay as long as the moon is full. Before she falls back into shadow and mystery… (*POPPY looks at him totally confused.*) Three days.

POPPY: The clowns were very funny.

RINGMASTER: Yes, if not somewhat unpredictable.

POPPY: Well, I thought it was very good. In fact this is unlike any circus I've ever seen before.

RINGMASTER: That is comforting to hear. Especially now that our time is drawing to an end.

POPPY: What do you mean?

RINGMASTER: Can you keep a secret, my dear? (*POPPY nods.*) The Cirque des Rêves is powered by magic.

POPPY: By magic? Don't be silly, there's no such thing.

RINGMASTER: How do you explain the strange things you have seen tonight, if not by magic?

POPPY: But it's all an illusion, isn't it?

RINGMASTER: Or is it the perfect cover?

He performs a spell for her, astonishing her into belief.

RINGMASTER: There are more things in heaven and on earth, than are dreamt of in your philosophy.

POPPY: But why are you stopping?

RINGMASTER: We live in a time of machines, my dear, a time of doubt. Magic is fading and we along with it.

POPPY: Is there nothing you can do?

RINGMASTER: There is one thing. A spell, that requires a series of items hidden within the circus. For years I have struggled to find them, but to no avail.

POPPY: And what happens if you don't find them?

RINGMASTER: We will all fade into nothing and magic will finally vanish, forever. Oh if only there was someone smart enough and brave enough with an appetite for adventure who would help us.

POPPY: Perhaps I could help you?

RINGMASTER: Oh, my dear, I could not ask such a thing of you!

POPPY: But I want to help.

RINGMASTER: It will not be easy. You will surely fail.

POPPY: Please let me try?

RINGMASTER: Well if you insist… The first clue. (*He hands her a card.*) You have until the final stroke of midnight two days from now. Solve the riddles, find the items, cast the spell… Good luck, Mademoiselle Parker, and may the fates be with you.

POPPY: (*Reading the card*) : This small disguise is plain to see,

> To hide away from you and me.

> Cut it off to spite your face,

> A crimson hole left in its place.

FATHER: I hope you had a pleasant evening, my dear.

POPPY: Oh very much so, Papa. There were two gentlemen with a life-sized doll and did the silliest / things…

FATHER: / Very interesting, I'm sure.

POPPY: Perhaps you could come with me tomorrow night and see it for yourself?

FATHER: Oh, no, I don't think so. I have quite enough excitement going on in my life right now. Professor Ludwig and myself are trying to introduce the Dewey Decimal System into the office and I needn't tell you but it is causing quite the coup!

POPPY: Oh father, if only you could/ have seen it all…

FATHER: /Shouldn't you be heading to bed, dear? Getting your beauty rest or whatever it is you ladies do?

POPPY: Father, if you saw the circus then maybe you would understand what I have been talking about. The excitement /of it all

FATHER:/Yes, yes, quite delightful, I'm sure.

POPPY: Papa. You really don't care do you?

FATHER: Oh yes, little dolls, delightful.

POPPY: Goodnight, Papa.

FATHER: Goodnight, Poppy.

NARRATOR 1: That night Poppy fell into a sleep deeper than she had in years.

NARRATOR 2: Images of the circus flooding into her mind, all the wonders she had seen that day filling her dreams.

NARRATOR 3: But at the same time she could not shake the warning of the fortune teller.

NARRATOR 1: Of darkness creeping in around her, of a shadow just out of sight.

NARRATOR 2: The feeling that there was now something watching her.

CECILY: Morning, Poppy.

POPPY: Hello, Cecily. Have you recovered from the excitement of last night?

CECILY: I think so, yes. Though heaven knows why the school felt it necessary for us to go.

POPPY: I'm going back tonight.

CECILY: My lord, why would you want to do that? Have you not lowered yourself to that of the common rabble enough for one lifetime?

POPPY: Oh, Cecily, I don't know if you could ever really understand.

CECILY: No, you're probably right.

TRISTAN: Morning, Poppy.

POPPY: Tristan!

TRISTAN: Morning, Cecily. (*She doesn't reply.*) Cecily. Cecily? Cecily, good morning!

CECILY: I'm not talking to you, Tristan.

TRISTAN: But you just did.

CECILY: Damn it, Tristan, must you always be so! (*She storms off.*)

TRISTAN: Sorry…

POPPY: I see you two didn't quite make up then.

TRISTAN: Not quite. Where were you?

POPPY: What do you mean?

TRISTAN: I waited for you, last night, but you never came back. We were supposed to walk home together.

POPPY: Oh no, I forgot.

TRISTAN: It's alright. I only waited for a couple of hours.

POPPY: Tristan, I am so sorry. You must think I'm terrible. I really didn't mean to forget you, I didn't, it's just that I got a little… distracted.

TRISTAN: I see. Sort of. Not really.

POPPY: You won't believe what happened there last night after I left you. (*The class bell begins to ring, interrupting them.*) Tristan, will you come with me tonight?

TRISTAN: You're going back?

POPPY: Yes, please come. I'll make it up to you for last night and you can help me with something.

TRISTAN: I dunno, Poppy…

POPPY: Please, Tristan. It will be worth it. I promise.

TRISTAN: Alright then. I will, if you swear you won't forget me again.

POPPY: I swear. (*She takes his hand. They leave.*)

NARRATOR 3: That day the only topic of conversation was that of the wonders that had been on display the night before.

NARRATOR 2: The town had never felt so alive, so full of possibility.

NARRATOR 1: Children walked to school with a notable spring in their step.

NARRATOR 3: Adults seemed marginally less disgruntled about the impending day of hardships that lay before them.

NARRATOR 1: And, for Poppy, it was as if the world had changed irrevocably. All she could do was count down the hours until nightfall when the circus would burst to life once more and the game would begin.

SONG 2: RINGMASTER SONG #2

You have watched your world begin to fall
To pieces past all hope or call
Now to lift your spirits and revive your soul
Mister Scaramantus please behold

Born between the sun and sky
With copper pennies on his eyes
He's been called from 'twixt the worlds
Deepest faith for to unfurl

Call it con or call it mystery
Seek in his gifts no earthly gain
To solve the riddles of the underworld
Would drive the mortal soul to flames

Cirque des Rêves

Call the dead to motion
O'erthrow the ocean
Bury all emotion
Kindly behold the show!

MR SCARAMANTUS is the animal tamer and magician, but he is falling apart, an alcoholic performer, no longer able to keep up the facade he needs. He performs a marvellous show with his assistant producing a lion at the end to be tamed. The lion breaks free and is about to go for the audience when Scaramantus hits it with a blow dart and it runs off. Scaramantus storms offstage disgruntled.

ASSISTANT: Ladies and gentlemen. Thank you for your… attention. We will now take a short break and will return with more sights and wonders than you can imagine… very soon. Thank you. (*She runs off.*)

POPPY: (*Spotting TRISTAN.*) You came!

TRISTAN: Of course I did. You asked me.

POPPY: We have to go backstage. I figured out the first clue. (*She shows him the clue.*) It's a clown's nose. Come on, they probably keep them in the dressing rooms.

TRISTAN: Poppy, wait. Why are you doing this?

POPPY: Because they need our help.

TRISTAN: But don't you feel it?

POPPY: What?

TRISTAN: I can't quite explain it. It's just… a feeling. There's something not right here.

POPPY: Don't be silly, Tristan. It's just your imagination. It's like our own little adventure, just you and me.

TRISTAN: Alright. I suppose it could be… fun?

One of the GRIMALDI BROTHERS appears with his red nose in his hand as if he is backstage getting ready. POPPY and TRISTAN follow him in. He is putting on make-up, humming to himself as he uses the audience as a mirror to apply the finishing touches. POPPY goes to try and steal his red nose.

GRIMALDI is about to discover POPPY so TRISTAN throws himself in the way as a distraction.

TRISTAN: Ahhhhhhh! Hello.

GRIMALDI: What are you doing here? Punters ain't supposed to be back here.

TRISTAN: I was… I'm just… such a big fan of yours! I wanted to see you in your natural habitat. But I realise that was now quite rude of me. Sorry for intruding.

GRIMALDI: A fan eh? Well I don't usually like people to see me in my skivvies but… Big fan, are you?

TRISTAN: Oh the biggest. Huge! I think you and your brother are the best thing in the entire circus. In any circus. Ever.

GRIMALDI: Really?

TRISTAN: But of course you're the real star of the show! It would all be nothing without you!

GRIMALDI: Well… you're not wrong there! God bless him, Dave's a good lad, but he doesn't have that little extra something, if you get me.

TRISTAN: Oh, yes, I totally agree.

GRIMALDI: Doesn't understand the finer nuances of what we do. Thinks it's all falling over and banging into things. He doesn't grasp the history, the weight of our type of craft.

TRISTAN: I couldn't have put it better myself.

GRIMALDI: Tradition! That's what it is. Here, I've got a few minutes before the next act if you fancy a tipple.

TRISTAN: Oh no, that's alright, I'm a bit young to have a drink.

GRIMALDI: Nonsense! Never too young to put hair on your chest. Plus this is a once in a lifetime offer! To have a drink with the Stephen Grimaldi, the superior of the Grimaldi Brothers!

TRISTAN: Oh… right… I… thank you… thank you very much.

GRIMALDI: (*He takes TRISTAN by the shoulders and leads him off.*) You can call me Steve by the way.

POPPY: (*She steps out from her hiding place and looks at the nose. She pulls a note out from inside it. Reading.*)

> Twist of time and turn of fate,
> to stop the clocks and slow the pace.
> It takes a key to wind up this heart,
> make the ticking stop before it falls apart…

POPPY: (*Considers a moment.*) The Living Doll! God, I am really good at these.

POPPY pockets the nose and the note. We find the doll set up at the back of the stage, inanimate. POPPY begins to examine around her, she turns the key in her back. The doll suddenly comes to life, repeating the song from earlier but this time it continues in full.

LIVING DOLL: SONG 3: LIVING DOLL MELODY

> So long ago upon a dream,
> A face a voice that haunts me still.
> A love untold, a passion filled,
> Lost upon the silver breeze.
> A flash of light left in its wake
> A crimson tide on a snow white face
> A prison full of broken souls,
> Held fast together for crimes untold.

She grabs POPPY.

> Be careful child, turn back, break free,
> This fate of ours is not for thee.
> Eternity is the soul price,
> To lose yourself in this prison of lies.

The ENTERTAINER appears and pulls the key out of the doll who collapses.

ENTERTAINER: Alright there, my little miss? Wandering around again, I see. Curious little thing, aren't you?

POPPY: (*Trying to pull herself back together, show that she's not afraid.*) I'm trying to help solve Mousier deWinter's riddles.

ENTERTAINER: Ah, the riddles! Of course.

POPPY: (*Looking at the scrap of paper, he reads it over her shoulder.*) I thought the winding key was the next piece but I don't think that's right…

ENTERTAINER: (*Mumbling to himself.*) No, it isn't the key you need. It's her heart.

POPPY: No, that can't be right.

ENTERTAINER: I'm afraid it is. You're gonna have to reach in there and pull it out if you want the next clue. Go on – she's just a machine and how can you hurt a machine?

POPPY: I don't think I can.

ENTERTAINER: What are we to do? (*Ponders a moment.*) Oh well, I suppose while I'm here I might as well help. (*He turns the doll to face him, reaches into her chest and as he grabs her heart she comes to life.*)

POPPY: Wait! No!

She breaths in sharply as if her lungs are taking in their last and she grabs on to him as he rips the clockwork heart from her chest. She collapses.

ENTERTAINER: There you are. (*He tosses the heart to her.*) Take care of that. Probably worth a few quid.

POPPY: What are you going to do to her?

ENTERTAINER: Don't worry. We have a place for all the old acts. This is her home, she isn't going anywhere. (*POPPY is frozen to the spot.*) Run along, my dear. You've still got one clue left, don't you? And time is running out.

He picks up the doll and goes.

RINGMASTER: Well, my girl, how are we getting on?

POPPY: Mousier, I think I've had enough.

RINGMASTER: Excuse me?

Cirque des Rêves

POPPY: I've enjoyed myself immensely and I'm so glad I could be of some help, but I think I better go home.

RINGMASTER: (*Becoming increasingly agitated.*) You cannot just walk away! We need you, Poppy. Only you can figure out the clues. I am sure of it!

POPPY: But I don't want to.

RINGMASTER: I don't care what you want, you will finish this and that is the end of it!

POPPY: No, I will not! Thank you for everything, Mousier, but I have made up my mind. I cannot help you anymore. Goodbye.

She leaves. RINGMASTER is left alone, at a loss as to what to do.

ENTERTAINER: Things not going entirely to plan, eh?

RINGMASTER: She's resisting.

ENTERTAINER: Strong willed is what you wanted, wasn't it?

RINGMASTER: We don't have time for this.

ENTERTAINER: Don't you worry, my old friend. I think I have a way to convince her to come back. She seems quite fond of that little friend of hers.

RINGMASTER: I don't care how you do it. Just get her back.

ENTERTAINER: Consider it done. Besides if she doesn't come back for him, he could be a handy little replacement for her.

RINGMASTER: One soul is not equal to another! We need her. I have told you what to do – now, just get it done.

ENTERTAINER: Whatever you say, 'boss'.

The following morning.

CECILY: Morning, Poppy. My lord, you look dreadful.

POPPY: Thank you for your sensitivity.

CECILY: I'm sorry. I'm just not used to seeing you so… but we all have our off days, I suppose.

POPPY: I couldn't sleep last night if you must know.

CECILY: Oh, well, yes, of course, I suppose you were worried. I don't think you need to be. I can't imagine he's gone very far, I mean he was never particularly bright.

POPPY: Cecily, what are you talking about?

CECILY: Tristan.

POPPY: What about him?

CECILY: He seems to have vanished.

POPPY: Tristan is missing? But I saw him last night.

CECILY: Well, you were probably the last one. He never went home. Can I ask was he acting strange at all? Did he seem like he was on the brink of doing anything drastic?

POPPY: No, he was just normal old Tristan. He came with me to… the circus.

MR KILLJAY: The what?

POPPY: The circus. They've taken him. Tristan was helping me, but we got separated and now they have him. Because I wouldn't play their game. We have to go back and save him.

MR KILLJAY: (*He considers her a moment.*) Miss Parker, I understand it has been a very stressful day but I think it's best we leave these matters to those better qualified and with less of an overzealous imagination.

POPPY: No, you don't understand. It was Mousier/ deWinter, the ringmaster.

MR KILLJAY: /I understand perfectly, my dear, and as whimsical as I find your need to deploy elaborate coping mechanisms, but sadly they are not going to help us find the boy. Off home with you this instant. Oh and, Poppy, no more stories. It really is getting rather tiresome.

POPPY: But Mr Killjay!

Cirque des Rêves

NARRATOR 2: Poppy was used to adults not taking her very seriously.

NARRATOR 1: She was accustomed to her father's dismissive remarks or mother's nonchalant shrugs. But those had always been over trivial matters. This was something else altogether.

NARRATOR 3: Sometimes when a person is faced with an impossible situation, they are forced to make impossible decisions.

NARRATOR 2: Poppy knew in her bones it was a trap. She had read enough adventure books to know that.

NARRATOR 3: But just like the heroes in her books she also knew that she had no choice. Her mind was made up and her will was set.

POPPY is at a loss as to what to do. She is looking around when the heart of the doll slowly starts to click. She looks for the cause of the noise and follows it to the LIVING DOLL who holds it in her hand. She is slumped and broken looking. POPPY tries and eventually stands her up. She puts the heart back into her chest.

POPPY: Hello? Can you hear me? I don't know why I'm asking you this, but... I need your help. Can you help me? Please. They've taken my friend. I don't know what to do...

The doll seems completely unresponsive. POPPY gives up and is walking away when:

LIVING DOLL: Poor Poppy Parker.

POPPY: You are alive, I knew it! Please, you have to help me. My friend, Tristan. They have him, don't they? Do you know where he is? I need to find a way / to get him...

LIVING DOLL: /Questions turn in that pretty head, but knowing answers may find you dead.

POPPY: What do you mean?

LIVING DOLL: Cursed not to live and never to die, held fast in this place by darkness and lies.

POPPY: I don't have time for more riddles. Give me a real answer.

LIVING DOLL: Hands of time and twist of fate, time runs out for you at this rate. A game to play. A prize to win. Only one way out once you are in.

POPPY: What happens if I don't solve the clues, give him what he wants? What happens to Tristan?

LIVING DOLL: A game to play. A prize to win.

POPPY: Tell me!

LIVING DOLL: A game to play. A prize to win.

POPPY: Why do you keep saying that!

LIVING DOLL: A game to play. A prize to win.

POPPY: This is hopeless. (*She realises what she has to do. Slowly she goes to the doll, she rips her heart out and the doll collapses. POPPY looks at the heart and takes out the final clue hidden inside. She is unfurling the clue and taking a breath in to read it when…*)

****

We jump back to Whitechapel.

GIRL: Hold on a minute. Can we just backtrack a bit here? Are you trying to tell me that the circus was actually full of ghosts instead of real people the entire time?

MR SPARROW: Yeah, that's it. Bit of a simplification but you've got the gist.

GIRL: That don't make no sense.

MR SPARROW: Yes, it does.

GIRL: No, it doesn't, cause if they're dead then why are they performing? Surely, if you're dead, you can't be doing things like juggling balls and that.

MR SPARROW: And how would you know? You ever been dead?

GIRL: No.

Cirque des Rêves

MR SPARROW: Well then, just shut your mouth and listen, will ya?

MR NIGHTINGALE: Patience, my dear Mr Sparrow, our young friend has some questions. This can only be expected from such a young underdeveloped mind. Please continue, my dear.

GIRL: Well, I'm just saying it's a bit odd. Like, do they get paid and all?

MR NIGHTINGALE: They don't work for the circus, poppet, they are the circus. They only perform to keep up the illusion, keep the magic alive. This is as close to living again that they will ever get. Plus when you're dead it ain't like you got much to be doing.

MR SPARROW: Yeah. Might as well put on a bit of a show. And ghosts love putting on a spectacle. Born showmen.

GIRL: (*Considers this a moment.*) Nah, I ain't buying it.

MR NIGHTINGALE: Well, that's the story regardless. Now do you want to hear the rest of it or not?

GIRL: Yeah, go on then. I've come this far, ain't I?

MR NIGHTINGALE: Right, so she's taking out the note and it's all mysterious and tension is really high and that, and it says…

****

POPPY: This trickster's game has no grain of truth,
look inside to find some proof.
The magician's crown is full of thorns,
take it back to break this conman's charms.

NARRATOR 1: Mr Scaramantus and his Menagerie of Wonders. For years it had been the most popular attraction at the circus.

NARRATOR 2: It had gathered a reputation for being filled with the most unusual creatures from all four corners of the earth.

NARRATOR 3: But over time things had fallen into disrepair. Many of the most stunning animals had escaped or been lost, and now Mr Scaramantus only had a handful of creatures to call his own.

NARRATOR 1: Not only that but his magic continued to fall away also. His tricks and illusions failing him at every turn.

NARRATOR 3: And what is a magician without his magic?

As POPPY walks through the menagerie, we hear the flutter of wings and the calls of the animals. She is looking around for the magician's hat and is looking at a particularly strange animal when Scaramantus enters:

MR SCARAMANTUS: I wouldn't get too close, my dear, he tends to bite.

MR SCARAMANTUS is a man at the end of his time. He is drunk and knows his days are numbered.

POPPY: What is he?

MR SCARAMANTUS: Some sort of cat, I think… I forget. Now what can I help you with? Come for an autograph, I assume? (*He takes off his magician's hat and places it down, picking up a bottle of something and begins to swig it. The hat is what POPPY needs and over the next section she continues to try and grab it while they talk.*)

POPPY: Actually I was hoping you could help me? I want to become a magician like you.

MR SCARAMANTUS: You do not want to become like me, girlie. This is no life for anyone.

POPPY: I was hoping you could teach me one small trick? Perhaps the one where you pull a rabbit out of your hat?

MR SCARAMANTUS: Don't be foolish child. Magic like that takes years to master. Card tricks on the other hand are child's play. Watch carefully. You are observing a master at work. (*Picks up a deck of cards.*) Pick a card, any card. (*POPPY does so.*) Memorise it. Got it? Excellent. Put it back. (*She puts it back in the deck. He shuffles the deck and places his hand on it and concentrates very hard. He pulls out a card.*) Is this your card? (*He holds up the devil card that scared the FORTUNE TELLER earlier. POPPY is shocked.*)

POPPY: No, but that's the card…

MR SCARAMANTUS: Oh bugger. (*He goes to shuffle the deck again and drops some cards. As he scrambles to pick them up, POPPY grabs the hat but she has nowhere to put it so just pops it on her head.*) Sorry about that I'm getting a bit… rusty. (*Spotting the hat.*) Were you always wearing that hat?

POPPY: Yes.

MR SCARAMANTUS: It looks a lot like mine.

POPPY: I got it made. Specially.

MR SCARAMANTUS: (*He looks at her a moment, considering his words.*) You know a magician's hat holds his power?

POPPY: Really? (*She tries to back away from him.*) I didn't know that. How fascinating.

MR SCARAMANTUS: Indeed. And if anyone was to try and take it from him… well. There's no knowing what he might do to protect such a thing.

POPPY: I see.

MR SCARAMANTUS: I think you better give me a look/ at that.

ASSISTANT: /Bob, how many times have I told you about leaving the cages… (*Spotting POPPY*) Oh.

MR SCARAMANTUS: What do you want?

ASSISTANT: You left the cages open. Again. I told you if you continue like this I'm gonna have to swap to another act.

MR SCARAMANTUS: For god sake, woman, don't you ever stop nagging?

ASSISTANT: I can't work under these conditions. I'm a trained actress, for god sake. There are plenty of other places my skills will be valued here.

MR SCARAMANTUS: Then go, you can be the assistant to the two Grimaldi dimwits. I hear their doll went caput!

ASSISTANT: (*He is swinging the bottle in front of her.*) You been drinking again.

MR SCARAMANTUS: What's it to you?

ASSISTANT: Give me that!

MR SCARAMANTUS: Hands off wench! (*They struggle with the bottle and the ASSISTANT pulls it from him and SCARAMANTUS falls over, bursting into fits of laughter. He is laughing hysterically but it is almost demented. There is something deeply tragic about him.*) I'm done! Finished! (*He continues to laugh manically.*)

ASSISTANT: I think you better go.

She makes to lift him back to his feet as POPPY runs away.

POPPY: Tristan! Oh thank God! (*She hugs him and realises that something is wrong.*) I promise I will get you out of here. (*She struggles to get him to his feet and is trying to carry him out when…*)

RINGMASTER: Mademoiselle Parker, I have been expecting you.

POPPY: What have you done to him?

RINGMASTER: A simple enchantment to keep him docile.

POPPY: Let him go.

RINGMASTER: I don't know if you are really in a position to be making demands, my dear.

POPPY: You have what you need, let us go.

RINGMASTER: That is not quite true. There is one other thing that the spell requires. (*Takes out a knife.*) A sacrifice.

POPPY: You lied.

RINGMASTER: I omitted, child, there is a difference. Every circus must have a Ringmaster. A soul to watch over it. My time is now up and we are in need of a successor.

POPPY: And what happens to you? You just get to walk away knowing you've trapped someone else here in your place.

Cirque des Rêves

RINGMASTER: I have paid my debt and eternal sleep shall be my reward.

POPPY: But he's just a boy.

RINGMASTER: As was I… (*The bells of midnight start to toll.*) Enough. The time is upon us. (*He places the hat with the items in front of him and takes out a knife. He holds out TRISTAN'S right hand and raises the knife.*) Spirits of a western isle, hear this call/ to now beguile…

POPPY: /Wait! I'll do it. I'll take your place. If you let him go.

RINGMASTER: You offer yourself freely?

POPPY: I do.

RINGMASTER: So be it, a trade. (*He offers her his hand to shake on it. She takes it and he pulls her towards him.*) Spirits of a western isle, hear this call to now beguile. To bind this prison, let no man walk free, take my offering, fulfill our decree! (*He takes the knife and chops off her finger. She screams and falls. As the ringmaster exits…*) You really are extraordinary, Miss Parker.

TRISTAN: Poppy? Poppy! Are you alright? I think you fainted. Father says that sometimes when women are overstimulated they can be prone to fits of hysteria and swooning.

POPPY: I'm fine, Tristan, thank you. (*He helps her up.*)

TRISTAN: I can't remember what happened, can you? One minute I was talking to that clown man and next thing I woke up here… Mother will be very annoyed.

POPPY: I'm sure she'll just be glad to see you.

TRISTAN: Right, well, it's late. Let me walk you home.

POPPY: Thank you, but I think I might just stay a little longer.

TRISTAN: Really? I don't know if you're really allowed…

POPPY: Go home. Tristan.

TRISTAN: Oh… right. I'll see you tomorrow, then. (*He starts to walk away.*)

POPPY: Tristan. (*She goes after him and gives him a kiss on the cheek and he instantly loses the ability to speak.*) Goodbye.

He leaves.

POPPY: Will I ever see him again?

STEVE GRIMALDI: That depends. We tend to come back full circle every now and again but I find that most of the people we met before are long gone.

POPPY: Maybe it's easier this way… It was a trap, wasn't it?

ENTERTAINER: More of test then a trap. And congratulations. You passed with flying colours.

STEVE GRIMALDI: You know there must be a better way of finding a new Ringmaster. All this running about, kidnapping children. Couldn't we just have an open audition next time or something?

ENTERTAINER: What are you talking about? It's tradition and who are you to mess with tradition?

POPPY: Enough.

ENTERTAINER: Yes ma'am. You know, I don't think we've ever had a female Ringmaster before. But we are nothing if not progressive. Welcome to the show, Poppy. I think you're really going to like it here.

They walk away, leaving her alone. She takes the magician's hat and puts it on.

POPPY: Me too.

NARRATOR 3: The next morning the circus had vanished without a trace. As if it had never been there at all.

NARRATOR 2: Poppy's disappearance sparked a countrywide search but no trace of her was ever found.

NARRATOR 1: The strange occurrences of that time fell into legend, whispers around the firelight, nothing more than ghosts in the dark.

NARRATOR 2: But sometimes, to this day, stories of a circus still emerge.

Cirque des Rêves

NARRATOR 1: A circus that seems to magically appear overnight.

NARRATOR 3: Full of strange and astonishing acts.

NARRATOR 2: And also there are rumours of its ringleader, a woman, who commands it all with four fingers on her right hand. A woman by the name of…

POPPY: Poppy Petunia Primrose Parker.

****

MR SPARROW: And there you have it, my little miss. That's what can happen to you if you get messed up with the so called 'circus' and the like. You're welcome.

MR NIGHTINGALE: Well, storytime is over. You better be running along. Lovely to meet you, my dear, best of luck with all your future endeavours.

GIRL: Is that it? That's the story that's supposed to scare me? That was rubbish.

MR SPARROW: How dare you. That was a well constructed, perfectly executed retelling of something some guy once told us in the pub.

GIRL: You just made all of that up, didn't you?

MR NIGHTINGALE: We might have embellished a little, but I promise it is as true as the day is long.

Clock begins to chime the hour.

MR NIGHTINGALE: Oh look at the time. You best be heading home. The sun will be up shortly and your folks will be awful sad to wake up and find you gone.

GIRL: I don't believe this. I've been standing here listening to you two go on and on and now it's too late. I'll never catch up with the circus!

MR SPARROW: What a pity.

GIRL: You've ruined everything. And don't think I don't know what you've been up to. As I said I ain't no fool.

She kicks MR SPARROW in the shin and storms off.

MR SPARROW: Ow! Why you little…

He goes to go after her, but MR NIGHTINGALE holds him back.

MR NIGHTINGALE: A pleasure to meet you, my dear. Safe home and may our paths one day cross again!

MR SPARROW: Well, that was a waste of time.

MR NIGHTINGALE: Oh contraire, my little friend. (*He removes an expensive looking pocket watch from his coat.*) My, my, my, I think daddy is not going to be too pleased with her when he finds out what his little darling has gone and lost on him.

They are both laughing when POPPY PARKER appears behind them.

POPPY: What you two laughing about? I thought I told you to pack this all up?

MR NIGHTINGALE: We were just attending to some business, Madame. But all done now.

POPPY: I should hope so. Get a move on. I want us out of this place by sun up.

MR NIGHTINGALE: Aye, aye captain.

POPPY: Oh and, Sparrow, you're messing up your entrance in the second act still. If you can't get it right tomorrow night, Nightingale gets to do the bit alone from now on.

MR SPARROW: But Poppy that /ain't fair!

POPPY: Excuse me?

MR SPARROW: Sorry, Mademoiselle Parker. I'll get it right, I swear.

POPPY: You better. There isn't any room in my circus for layabouts. You can be replaced. Remember that.

She exits.

MR SPARROW: Why's she always picking on me?

MR NIGHTINGALE: You got one of them faces.

MR SPARROW: Oh right, yeah, fair enough.

They pack up their stuff. They start singing as they work.

MR SPARROW & MR NIGHTINGALE:

> SONG 4: LORD LANDLESS
>
> Oh whither away Lord Landless said she,
> My mossy banks why pass over.
> Maiden, the landless must wanderer be,
> No world is too wide for the rover.
> Heigh ho onwards I go,
> No world is too wide for the rover.

POPPY PARKER enters and mournfully sings along.

> A-walking went she,
> With Landless and free,
> O'er highways and byways they travelled.
> Weary maid down by the brink of the sea
> She sleepeth on green grey gravel.
> Heigh ho! heart full of woe
> She sleepeth on green grey gravel.
>
> Heigh ho! heart full of woe,
> She sleepeth on green grey gravel.

They leave.

THE END

All honey

Ciara Elizabeth Smyth

First produced at the New Theatre, Dublin, in September 2017, as part of the Dublin Fringe Festival. Subsequently produced at Bewley's Café Theatre in January 2018.

DIRECTOR: Jeda de Brí
SET DESIGNER: Sinéad Purcell
LIGHTING DESIGNER: Maggie Donovan
COSTUME DESIGNER: Ellen Therese Fleming
STAGE MANAGER: Sionnán Ni Nualláin
PRODUCTION ASSISTANT: Tamar Keane
PRODUCER: Ciara Elizabeth Smyth

CHARACTERS & CAST:
MAE: Ashleigh Dorrell
LUKE: David Fennelly
RU: Danielle Galligan
BARRY: Keith Jordan
VAL: Ciara Elizabeth Smyth

Ciara Elizabeth Smyth is a playwright from Dublin. *All honey* won the Fishamble New Writing Award in 2017. During 2018, her play, *Pacemaker*, was shortlisted for Fishamble's A Play for Ireland initiative and she was Writer in Residence in The New Theatre. She presented *We Can't Have Monkeys in the House* as her residency production, which then transferred to the Peacock Stage in August 2019 for the inaugural Young Curators Festival. Ciara was also selected for the Rough Magic SEEDS Programme 2018-2020 and to participate in Abbey Works 2019 in the Abbey Theatre.

SCENE I:

Her Nightgown

RU is unpacking a box hurriedly, looking for something, muttering to herself. LUKE enters, slightly flustered and pauses briefly, as if he had forgotten what he came in for. When he opens the door we hear the murmur of people and music from down the hall. A house-warming party.

RU stops what she is doing and stares at LUKE. Buzzer sounds and LUKE leaves the room to answer it. She finds what she is looking for, gets up, glances in a mirror and leaves the room. Stage is empty for about 8 seconds. Muffled sound of RU and another female talking. Door flies open. MAE walks in, holding a depleted gin & tonic, followed by RU.

MAE: The fact is, it's happening.

RU: Right.

MAE: I mean, that's just a fact. The fact is. It's happening.

RU: Is it?

MAE: It is. (*Pause.*) I mean, I felt it. He would. Deny. Denied. Everything. I thought I was going out of my mind. In my head he was… at it. Then in the flesh, I was. Accusing him unjustly.

RU: Mmmm.

MAE: But then I found it.

RU: What?

MAE: (*Whispers.*) Her nightgown.

RU: Her nightgown?

MAE: Her nightgown. Can you believe it?

RU: No.

MAE: I know.

RU: That's so strange.

MAE: Isn't it? (*Nodding. Pause.*) Is it?

RU: It's just. A nightgown?

MAE: Oh.

RU: Right?

MAE: There's no need to be embarrassed.

RU: Sorry?

MAE: You see, Ru, it's a gown. That you wear. When you sleep. In the night-times.

RU: No, no, I know what a nightgown is.

MAE: So what's the problem?

RU: You found her nightgown?

MAE: Yes, well.

RU: The woman you think is sleeping with your –

MAE: Yes.

RU: Her nightgown, you found.

MAE: Alright, Ru, can we pick this up, please?

RU: My problem is, if this woman is... (*gesturing*) with your... Sorry, what are we calling him now?

MAE: Barry.

RU: Just Barry?

MAE: My Barry.

All honey

RU: (*Pause.*) Okay. If she is, if she has been, with your Barry, in your house. She's not. Staying the night. I mean she wouldn't sleep over.

MAE: No, of course not. I live there.

RU: That's right.

MAE: That's where I sleep.

RU: Of course.

MAE: And I don't have a guest room.

RU: You don't.

MAE: What are you getting at, Ru?

RU: So if she's not staying over, in the night-times.

MAE: Because I sleep in my bed.

RU: Because you sleep in your bed. So if she's not staying over in the night-times, because you sleep in your bed. Then why should she need a nightgown?

MAE: Oh, yes, I see what you're saying.

RU: You do.

MAE: Yes, of course. Because they would be engaging in intercourse.

RU: Well. Sex.

MAE: Language, Ru.

RU: And also.

MAE: Hmm?

RU: A nightgown?

MAE: Yes?

RU: Who wears a nightgown?

MAE: Ahm.

RU: I mean I don't wear a nightgown.

MAE: No.

RU: I sleep naked.

MAE: What?

RU: Nude.

MAE: Right.

RU: So?

MAE: (*Pause.*) I mean. I wear pyjamas.

RU: No!

MAE: What?

RU: You found the nightgown.

MAE: Yes, I did!

RU: And what did you think?

MAE: Well, what would you think? If you found a nightgown in Luke's things?

RU: (*Pause.*) The neighbours.

MAE: What?

RU: We share a washing machine. With the neighbours.

MAE: Ru, how is that helpful? I have my own washing machine.

RU: Of course.

MAE: And my own house.

RU: Yep.

MAE: That I bought. That he stays in.

RU: Rent free. I know, I'm sorry, go on. You found the nightgown.

MAE: Yes. And this nightgown. More than confirmed my suspicions.

All honey

RU: I suppose it would.

MAE: It did.

RU: Prick.

MAE: Skirt chaser.

RU: (*Pause.*) Was it. Very sexy?

MAE: It was… (*Remembering*) horrific.

RU: Oh, Mae.

MAE: It was so frilly. You couldn't move for the frills.

RU: Jesus.

MAE: High neck, long sleeves, floor length. Baggy, too. My God was it baggy.

RU: Oh. That's sort of different than I –

MAE: I mean I presumed they were playing house or some sick –

RU: (*Nodding seriously.*) Right.

MAE: – Thing.

RU: Mmm.

MAE: In nightgowns with Victorian fetish –

RU: Uh.

MAE: – Shit.

RU: Mmm.

MAE: All like… (*Makes a face and gestures.*)

RU: Perverts.

MAE: (*Nodding slowly and inhaling before speaking.*) Exactly. (*Pause.*) So I confronted him. I smell her off you. You're found out. Caught. In your lies. No fools here, baby.

RU: Baby?

MAE: No fools! Did you think I wouldn't find out? You scum. The colour drained from his face.

RU: And?

MAE: He crumbled. (*Nodding.*) Buried his face between my legs. Clutched at the back of my thighs. Shaking. Like a…. (*Silence as both RU and MAE think of an appropriate simile.*)

RU: Like a dog?

MAE: Yes. Like a dog. Shaking like a dog. He shook like a dog.

RU: Wow. So he?

MAE: Hmm?

RU: Admitted.

MAE: What? No.

RU: What?

MAE: No.

RU: He didn't?

MAE: I made a mistake. I … (*pause*) when he had his face buried, and I was… (*Ru makes a talking gesture with her hand.*) You are being so unhelpful.

RU: Sorry.

MAE: When I was… going on. A bit. I mentioned the nightgown. I said it out. I've found her nightgown! When the last syllable left my lips. His grip on my thighs loosened. And I knew I'd made a mistake. Nightgown? he said. And he said it like that, too. Nightgown? Then the laughter started. That fucked me right off. Then he looked up at me. Tears in his eyes. But not good tears, not the tears I wanted. Bad tears, happy tears. The nightgown. he said, the nightgown is for my mother.

RU: What? Was it new?

MAE: Yes.

RU: It had tags?

MAE: Indeed.

RU: In a shopping bag?

MAE: Precisely. (*Brief pause.*)

RU: What?

MAE: That's not important. You see I caught him.

RU: Did you?

MAE: He broke down. Why did he break down?

RU: Okay. What did you say?

MAE: Nothing. At first. Couldn't believe he was smiling. Then I started. I mean, I really got started. I told him he hasn't been showing me any affection. I said to him, I'm a success. This is what success looks like. These are the eyes, nose, mouth and ears of success. Quite literally, this is the face of success. And if you think such a success is going to hang around for cold scraps of meat that you try to pass off for affection, think again, baby.

RU: Baby? Again –

MAE: He apologised. Said he would. Try.

RU: Right. That sounds.

MAE: Yeah.

RU: Did you ask why he got so upset?

MAE: I was out of ammo at that stage. So we went to bed. He was gone when I woke up. And guess what he took with him.

RU: No?

MAE: The nightgown. To work.

RU: When was that?

MAE: Two days ago.

RU: Where is he now?

MAE: He was supposed to meet for dinner and come here together.

RU: And why didn't he?

MAE: He texted. He had to work late. Emergency. Said he'll be here in a few hours.

RU: Jesus.

MAE: I know what you're thinking.

RU: Do you?

MAE: Yes, I do. When is Detective Mae going to re-confront that bastard Barry.

RU: I wasn't thinking that at all.

MAE: I'm going to call him out. Again. Tonight. In front of everybody. Genevieve said it would be cathartic.

RU: Genevieve told you to do that? Here?

MAE: She did. She's so smart.

RU: You might like some privacy?

MAE: No, I'd like the audience.

RU: Okay, why don't we first get a drink?

MAE: Another one. Yes.

RU: Yes. Another one. And let's have a chat about that option.

They both go to leave, MAE first. As she exits, enter LUKE.

LUKE: Ru, oh hi, Mae. Having a good time?

MAE: (*Sarcastically.*) Oh yes, Luke. I am having a brilliant time.

LUKE: (*Pause.*) Great. Ru?

RU: Luke?

LUKE: Would you go out and serve please, I just need to –

RU: Sure, no problem. (*RU starts looking at LUKE with wild eyes and signalling she would like to talk to him. LUKE picks up on this.*)

LUKE: Eh, Mae?

MAE: Yes, Luke?

LUKE: I think someone. Was… at… your handbag. All your lady bits are on the floor.

MAE: What?

LUKE: Yeah, all over the place. Someone really got in there. You better go… have a look.

MAE: Jesus, Luke. (*MAE leaves quickly. LUKE, pleased with his quick thinking, turns to RU.*)

SCENE II:
You Detached Yourself

RU: What was that?

LUKE: I thought you wanted me to get her out.

RU: I did, but I didn't want you to say someone robbed her bag.

LUKE: I thought that was good.

RU: It wasn't.

LUKE: Yeah, well, I'm not good on the spot and I'm not good at pretending.

RU: I can see that.

LUKE: Is everything okay?

RU: Not really.

LUKE: (*Looking at his phone.*) Right.

RU: Luke.

LUKE: (*Looking up from his phone.*) Sorry, people keep texting me.

RU: We have a problem.

LUKE: Right. Is it –

RU: Barry.

LUKE: What about him?

RU: He's been having an affair.

LUKE: What makes you think that?

RU: Well, Mae thinks that.

LUKE: Oh. I thought they broke up.

RU: They're back together.

LUKE: Really? He didn't, I mean he never. Said.

RU: You were talking to him about it?

LUKE: No, just. You know. We chat. And he never. Mentioned.

RU: Well they are. But now –

LUKE: When?

RU: When what?

LUKE: Sorry, since when are they back together?

RU: Two weeks.

LUKE: Right.

RU: Am I missing something?

LUKE: No. Sorry no.

RU: You're anxious.

All honey

LUKE: No. I'm distracted. I just. He's coming here tonight.

RU: Yeah that's the problem. Did he say anything to you when you were out with him last week?

LUKE: No, Jesus, no.

RU: Right. Well. She's planning a confrontation tonight. Here.

LUKE: Here?

RU: Yes.

LUKE: Who is she confronting?

RU: What? Barry.

LUKE: Yes, of course, sorry. (*Pause.*) And who does she. Think he's. Been with…?

RU: She doesn't know.

LUKE: She must have some idea. (*Brief pause.*)

RU: Luke, do you have some idea?

LUKE: I don't, Jesus, not at all. It's just. I didn't think we'd have to stop a fight tonight.

RU: I know. She found a nightgown the other night and it's really set her off. (*Pause.*)

LUKE: A nightgown?

RU: A nightgown. She thought it was his lover's. But, apparently, it was a present for his mother.

LUKE: Right. Where is she now?

RU: Gone to get a drink.

LUKE: You thought that was the best thing? Alcohol?

RU: Yes.

LUKE: You should go out to her.

RU: I will. (*RU goes to leave and stops before LUKE can follow her.*)

RU: How is everything out there?

LUKE: Fine, yeah.

RU: Are people enjoying themselves?

LUKE: Oh yeah. They seem to be. Loving it.

RU: Nothing… strange or wonderful?

LUKE: No. Oh. There's a girl just come in with some serious… (*Searching for the word.*) Eyebrows.

RU: Oh yeah. That's Jessica. From work.

LUKE: Jessica?

RU: (*Doing an impression of her.*) Jessica.

LUKE: Oh your one.

RU: Yeah.

LUKE: Do you hang round with her?

RU: Yeah, tea break, lunch.

LUKE: She's mental. She just told me she broke up with someone because of the stock market.

RU: Yeah. Did she start to explain how the stock market works?

LUKE: Yes! Ru, I don't want to know how the stock market works.

RU: I know, it's awful. (*RU smiles.*) I love you.

LUKE: I love you too. (*Silence.*)

RU: Do you? (*Silence.*)

LUKE: Of course. (*Silence.*)

RU: Okay. (*Pause.*) Good. (*RU goes to say something but decides not to. Pause.*) You do love me.

LUKE: I do.

RU: Okay. No, I know. It's just. You say. Nothing.

LUKE: I… don't?

RU: You don't love me?

LUKE: I do!

RU: Okay. You don't ever say.

LUKE: I just said.

RU: Yeah. But other things. You don't ever say other things. Voluntarily.

LUKE: (*Kindly.*) You're not making sense.

RU: Okay.

LUKE: I do love you. Sweet. Pea.

RU: How much do you love me?

LUKE: Bloody loads.

RU: As much as I love you?

LUKE: Probably.

RU: What?

LUKE: Yes, yes.

RU: (*Under her breath.*) Unsettling.

LUKE: Pardon?

RU: (*Much louder.*) That's unsettling. (*Silence.*)

LUKE: We should go back out.

RU: Why?

LUKE: Because you're getting all. Raaah. You know the way you get.

RU: No.

LUKE: Ah, you do know.

RU: Nope.

LUKE: Ah, you know the way you are.

RU: Are you confident continuing this?

LUKE: No, I'd really like to stop talking.

RU: Good. (*Pause.*) Do you know what, I had a dream last night about you.

LUKE: Did you?

RU: I did. I was outside my old office with the people from my old office and the sun was shining. Like it does. In the summer. Do you remember? It was beside the Liffey. So the sun was shining and hitting the water and I looked down at the water and the water was blue. Can you believe it? Because it's normally –

LUKE: Yeah.

RU: Green.

LUKE: What?

RU: (*Louder.*) Green.

LUKE: Green.

RU: Yes. Well. I can't remember exactly what I was doing, but I was on a mission. Then, all of a sudden, I hear an electrical wheelchair.

LUKE: What's that?

RU: An electrical wheelchair.

LUKE: Right. No yeah, that's, that's what I thought you said.

RU: Yeah. (*Pause.*) So I hear an electrical wheelchair. And it's coming at me. Fast. And I looked up and it was you. In the electrical wheelchair. And you were going. So fast. And you flew right past me, in your chair, and you went straight into the water. Then you detached yourself from the chair and swam to the side. You climbed out and ran over to me and said, 'I didn't want you to be late.' Isn't that sweet?

All honey

LUKE: Is it?

RU: Yeah. You didn't want me to be late.

LUKE: For what?

RU: My mission.

LUKE: Right. (*Pause.*) Sounds like Luke deserves a thank you.

RU: Yes, I would thank you but I think you were having an affair.

LUKE: What?

RU: In the dream. In the dream you were having an affair.

LUKE: What? When?

RU: When what?

LUKE: When was I having an affair on you? I was flying around in a wheelchair.

RU: (*Remembering.*) Oh you were going so fast.

LUKE: When was I... 'doin it' on you? I was in a wheelchair.

RU: Oh you don't think people in wheelchairs can cheat?

LUKE: No. Logistically.

RU: What?

LUKE: Logistically. Was I 'at it'? When I was in the wheelchair? Was she on my lap?

RU: No, no, before that I think.

LUKE: Did you see?

RU: No. I didn't see, it was just a feeling I got.

LUKE: Was she as good looking as you?

RU: It wasn't with a woman.

LUKE: What?

RU: It wasn't with a woman.

LUKE: Okay. Was he. As good looking as you?

RU: It was a penguin.

LUKE: A what?

RU: A penguin.

LUKE: A penguin?

RU: Yes.

LUKE: I was cheating on you with a penguin?

RU: That's right.

LUKE: But you didn't see any of this.

RU: Correct.

LUKE: You just got the feeling I'd been cheating on you with a penguin before I whizzed past you in an electrical wheelchair that I didn't need?

RU: That was the state of affairs, yes.

LUKE: That's horrible.

RU: I don't think you'd really cheat on me.

LUKE: No.

RU: It was just a dream.

LUKE: No, that you think I'd... force myself upon a penguin.

RU: I don't think you'd force yourself upon a penguin!

LUKE: But you said –

RU: No it was more emotional. Hand holding.

LUKE: They don't have hands. They have –

RU: Yeah.

LUKE: I'd never do that to you.

RU: I don't think you would, love.

LUKE: Right. Good. (*Pause.*) Is something wrong?

RU: Yes.

LUKE: Is it the penguin?

RU: No.

LUKE: Oh. What is it? Cup. Cake.

RU: I know you're trying to be affectionate using those names but you just sound hungry.

LUKE: I'm starving.

RU: I spent all day cleaning while you sat there on your phone. And when I asked you to clean the baking tray you threw it in the bin.

LUKE: It was very dirty though.

RU: That's why I asked you to clean it. Luke, you can't spend all day looking at your phone. We're together all the time now. You have to talk to me.

LUKE: Okay. I didn't realise I was. I'm sorry.

RU: Okay. Let's go outside.

LUKE: Hang on, where is the thing that holds the dip? That's what I came in for. Some guys from your work just came in. They brought parfait.

RU: Paté or parfait?

LUKE: What's the difference?

RU: Luke, come on.

LUKE: Okay?

RU: Are they all here? The dip thing is in the small box.

LUKE: Oh. Good. Not all of them, are they all coming? And where's the thing that holds the thing that holds the dip?

RU: They are. It's in the big box.

LUKE: Where is it?

RU: In there. It should be right on top.

LUKE: Ehh.

RU: It's right there.

LUKE: (*Talking over her.*) It's right where? Here?

RU: Yes.

LUKE: Oh, right, no, yes, I mean the other thing.

RU: Oh, that broke.

LUKE: Oh.

RU: Yeah. There should be another thing though.

LUKE: Forget it. Are your friends from fencing coming?

RU: Yeah, I think so.

LUKE: Great.

RU: There'll be loads. We're so popular.

LUKE: We're not really.

RU: Luke, I know.

LUKE: Oh yeah. I hope the lads don't bring –

RU: I can't stand her.

LUKE: I did tell them not to. (*Buzzer sounds.*)

LUKE: Will I get that?

RU: Someone else will get it.

LUKE: It is our apartment.

RU: Yes, but we invited them to our apartment.

LUKE: I don't follow.

RU: We put the heating on. The least they could do is get the door.

LUKE: I didn't put the heating on. (*Silence. Buzzer sounds again.*)

RU: You didn't put the heating on?

LUKE: I. Yeah, no, I'll get that. You leave six seconds after me. (*With a smile.*) So people don't think I was forcing myself upon you.

RU: Like rape?

LUKE: Ru!

RU: Were you going to rape me?

LUKE: No!

RU: Luke, did you intend to rape me?

LUKE: (*Almost shouting.*) I did not INTEND to rape you. (*Silence.*)

RU: That didn't sound great.

LUKE: It did not. (*Buzzer goes again.*) Yeah, I'll get that.

RU smiles. LUKE leaves. RU stands, staring after him. She makes for the door but then remembers where the other thing is located. Sounds of people entering. She goes to a box near the corner of the room and takes out another thing that holds the thing that holds the dip. As she does the door flies open and in walks VAL wearing a tiger mask.

SCENE III:

Have You Taken Leave Of Your Senses?

VAL closes the door behind her. She looks around the room but doesn't see RU. She tears her mask off, throws it and her bag on a chair. She then rips her coat off and stands in the centre of the room. She pauses before she speaks. RU is frozen in horror as the exact person she did not want at her party has just walked in. She does not want VAL to see her. VAL begins to practise laughing.

VAL: (*Laughing.*) Oh, you are a riot, Tiernan! Such interesting and sexy facts you know about nature... Oh. Hello. I'm actually having a conversation with my new friend here. Who is he? He's new and you don't know him. What's that? Oh, you want a 'quiet word' in the box room with me? Well, I'm busy. Ah, ah, you made yourself quite clear last night. *Please, Val, I love you.* Do you? Well, I don't. I can safely say there's no love, no love of any kind, between us. It's alright, Tiernach, I have this under control. I know how to deal with. This. How dare you? You think you can just swan in to this soirée and bend down on your bent knee and offer me the moon? You have another thing coming to you, pally. Sorry, who do you think you are? I don't care if you can't breathe without me, I'm not your goddamn inhaler. No, that wasn't a stab at your dust allergy. Listen, hey. Shut up. I'm not the kind of girl who responds to threats, or pleas or... Or cakes or sandwiches or whatever else you have to throw at me. In the buffet of life, I am not a sandwich. You are looking at sushi. Do you have any idea how difficult sushi is to construct? Hmm? What, you think you're some sort of sushi architect? I. Am. Sushi. Diamond sushi. And no. You can't just pick sushi up, bring it for a day out in the sun and leave it in a hot car with no windows rolled down. Because I'll tell you this, and I mean it, that sushi that you loved. That sushi will poison you. It will poison you dead. Oh stop crying, we all have tear ducts. You're making a scene. You're a stranger to me now, do you hear me, a stranger. Oh, hello stranger, lovely to meet you, I'm Val and I'm fantastic. No, I don't know you. I know Tiernachnamach, my new friend, my new gentleman caller. He's been there for me through thick and thin. And they have been the most sensual 17 minutes of my life. Get up off your knees, you bin. It's over, do you hear me? Do you understand now, it's over!

VAL turns around to leave and spots RU. RU has been engrossed in VAL's speech and lets out a shriek when VAL clocks her. They both get a fright.

VAL: Ru, what are you doing... are you following me?

RU: What? No –

VAL: Sliding into rooms after me –

RU: No, I wasn't –

All honey

VAL: Staring at me, drooling, taking note of my figure –

RU: Val, I live –

VAL: (*Gasps.*) You fancy me.

RU: No!

VAL: Then why are you in here with your pants down?

RU: They're not down.

VAL: Well, not now.

RU: Val –

VAL: Lust, Ru, gets us all in the end.

RU: (*Raising her voice.*) Val. I live here.

VAL: There is really no need to shout.

RU: I'm sorry.

VAL: That's fine.

RU: (*Pause.*) Okay. What are you. Doing? Here.

VAL: Have you had your hair done?

RU: What?

VAL: Your hair. You've had it done.

RU: Oh. Yeah, yes, I suppose I have had it. Done.

VAL: Yes, the last time I saw you, it was –

RU: Up.

VAL: Red. (*They look at each other suspiciously.*) It's terribly nice.

RU: Oh, thank you.

VAL: Terribly nice, indeed.

RU: Thank… you. (*Silence.*)

VAL: So you and Barry, how are you and Barry?

RU: Luke.

VAL: That's what I said.

RU: You said Barry.

VAL: No, I didn't.

RU: Yes. You said Barry. Do you know Barry?

VAL: You are mistaken, I said Luke. I did not say Barry. I did not say whatever you are saying I said. You are putting words in my mouth because Barry was not the word I used. Okay? The word I used, the person I said was Luke. I said Luke. You are going out with Luke and I said Luke. (*Door opens, LUKE enters.*)

LUKE: Ru, are you still in here? – Oh shit.

VAL: Hello, Luke.

LUKE: Val's here.

RU: Val's here.

VAL: And Ru was in here. Watching me. It was weird.

LUKE: Ru, Val's here.

VAL: You might have to keep an eye on that.

RU: I can see that.

VAL: Looks like she might be a gay. For me.

LUKE: Val, yeah, yes. Val. I didn't see you come in. Did you come in with…?

VAL: The lads.

LUKE: Which ones?

VAL: All of them.

LUKE: Right but specifically?

VAL: Michael?

All honey

LUKE: No, sorry, he's not here yet.

VAL: That's okay.

RU: Luke.

LUKE: Val.

VAL: Mmm?

LUKE: You don't have a drink. Can I get you a drink?

VAL: This is different to your last place, Luke.

LUKE: Yes. It's a different place.

VAL: Oh, is that it?

LUKE: Yes, it's not the same place.

VAL: Oh, yes, that's it. I was at your last place, see.

RU: Yes. You were.

VAL: I was. I was at your last place at your last party. Do you remember? Her hair was.

RU: Up.

VAL: Red.

LUKE: Yes, we remember. (*Laughing nervously.*) You weren't a big fan of my glasses.

VAL: Your what?

RU: Luke's glasses. You broke –

VAL: Luke doesn't wear glasses.

RU: Luke's wine glasses.

VAL: Oh, yes, that's right. Your glasses. Your wine glasses. I had a little accident and broke one.

RU: Seven.

VAL: Pardon?

RU: (*Smiling.*) Seven.

VAL: (*Laughing.*) I don't think it was seven.

RU: (*Still smiling.*) No, it was. It was seven.

VAL: (*Laughing.*) No, I don't think it was seven.

RU: (*Still smiling.*) Definitely. A set of six and a spare one.

VAL: (*Forcing laughter.*) Well, I don't think old Ruey here has the best memory!

RU: (*Feigning laughter.*) I may not have remembered your name but I remember the glasses.

VAL: (*Immediately halting any smile or laughter.*) And I suppose you're looking for reparations, hmm? I suppose that's why you invited me to this party? To skim my wallet. I suppose that's why Ru asked for a quiet word in the box room, to corner me for money!

RU: What the fuck?

LUKE: Oh my God.

VAL: Well, let me get my goddamn chequebook out. (*VAL picks up her bag and takes a cheque book and a pen out of it. She begins aggressively scribbling in the book.*)

RU: Out. I want you out.

LUKE: Ru, get her out.

VAL: Hang on, ladies and gentlemen, wait til old Val ponies up the dough! We're down wine glasses, seven of them, seven she says. We've been drinking our Super Valu swill from cups, mugs, leaves that we've fashioned into goblets. Sometimes our hands. We cup our goddamn hands together and sup and pray that no wine escapes. And you know why? Because Val broke all our wine glasses! Because Val destroyed all our receptacles. Because Val ruined our lives. Well, here's your blood money, Ru, here's your recompense. The bone's dry, Ru, the marrow's gone, baby. (*VAL rips a cheque off the book and hands it to RU. RU stands still, breathing calmly. LUKE is frozen on the other side of the room.*)

LUKE: Baby?

RU: I won't say it again.

VAL: Well, no wait, read the cheque.

RU: I won't say it again.

VAL: No, hang on, you'll like this. Give it a. Read.

RU: You'll be leaving my house now.

VAL: Read the cheque, Ru.

RU: Have you taken leave of your senses, get the fuc –

VAL: Read the fucking cheque, Ru.

RU stares at VAL for a moment. VAL smiles at her. RU then looks down to read the cheque.

VAL: Out loud.

RU: (*Reading.*) Pay: Ru & Luke, my squishiest friends. Sum of One Hundred & Fifty Glasses Only. For services rendered. Val… Then she's just drawn a winky face. (*VAL erupts in a fit of laughter.*)

VAL: Your faces. Your… (*Laughing.*) That isn't even a real cheque book.

RU: (*Reading.*) The Bank of Sass

VAL: You should have seen. Who writes cheques? (*Wiping tears from the outer corners of her eyes.*) Oh. Wow.

LUKE: That was. A good. One. Val.

VAL stops laughing and stares at LUKE. All three freeze for a moment. VAL looks like she's ready to pounce, as does RU. LUKE looks like he may faint.

VAL: I know, Luke.

RU: Drink! Drink. You have no drink. How ru-rude of us.

VAL: Well, you said it, not me, Ru Rude! Is this a bedroom?

RU: Not at the moment.

VAL: Because there's no bed?

RU: Because there's no bed.

VAL: Hmm. Not what I would have done.

LUKE: Val, red or white?

VAL: (*Gesturing at RU's hair.*) I was positive it was red.

LUKE: Wine, wine, the wine. Red or white wine.

VAL: Oh the wine, yes, I'd like some wine.

LUKE: Okay, after you.

VAL: Ooh here's your twin, Ru. Luke can't wait to get me all lubed up. You'd like that, too, wouldn't you, Ru? You could have your way with me again.

RU: There is no again, I didn't do it the first time.

VAL: Only cause I caught you. If I'd have known you were both so eager, I would have worn one of my saucy nightgowns.

RU starts. She stares at VAL. RU and LUKE stare at each other.

VAL: What… why are you looking at each other?

LUKE: After you, Val!

VAL: Oh, he's mad for it! Follow us into the bedroom, Ru.

LUKE shoots a terrified look at RU as he leaves the room with VAL. As they go out, MAE comes in, carrying her handbag. VAL and MAE stare at each other momentarily.

SCENE IV:
His 25 Best Qualities

MAE: Hello.

VAL: Oh. Hello.

MAE: Do I know you?

VAL: When did you get here?

All honey

MAE: About 8. Have we met?

VAL: Never. Did you come alone?

MAE: Excuse me?

VAL: Alone, alone… did you come alone?

LUKE: Wine, wine, remember wine? Okay, out we go.

VAL: Lovely to see you. (*LUKE and VAL leave the room. MAE stares after VAL.*)

MAE: Who's she? (*MAE stares after the door for a moment then sits and puts her head in her lap.*)

RU: (*Whispering.*) Baby? Nightgown? Barry. Barry. (*MAE looks up at RU.*)

MAE: What?

RU: Nothing.

MAE: What have I done, Ru? I've been a fool.

RU: I beg your pardon?

MAE: I've pushed him away. That's why he's acting so strange.

RU: But Mae, earlier –

MAE: Earlier Mae was crazy. I've just been talking to Genevieve.

RU: Jesus. You called her? It's 9 o'clock.

MAE: She doesn't mind. She made me see that I was acting insane.

RU: What did she say?

MAE: She said, Mae, you're acting insane.

RU: Did she?

MAE: Yes. She's really got her head screwed on. She said I don't know how to be happy.

RU: Right.

MAE: Ru. Think about it. He has never done anything to make me distrust him.

RU: He has done, literally, loads of things.

MAE: He's a wonderful man. So many qualities. His twenty-five best qualities. One, he's genuinely funny. Two, he's intelligent. Three, he's graceful, such grace for a man, you've never seen such grace. He moves like a dream. Four, spontaneous, five, explosive, six, terrific looking…

RU: He's not terrific looking.

MAE: Seven, a tease.

RU: Can you not do the full twenty-five?

MAE: How can I not? He's perfect.

RU: Okay. Maybe. Let's talk about Barry. The first time you spent the night together, you had an epileptic fit and he went downstairs and ate ice cream until you stopped.

MAE: He thought I was having a nightmare.

RU: That's not better.

MAE: Why are you being so negative, you're usually so diplomatic. I made a mistake with the nightgown. I'm seeing things that aren't there.

RU: I'm not sure that you are. He's not… exactly… brilliant.

MAE: Come off it, Ru. He's perfect. I'm ruining our love, aren't I? I constantly feel like he's going to find someone better than me. I'm so anxious all the time. I need to see Genevieve. She calms me. Can I invite her here please?

RU: I would just really rather if you didn't invite your therapist to our housewarming.

MAE: It's an apartment and she's a life coach.

RU: Okay –

MAE: Ru, please. You don't understand. Just stop… this has just gotten out…out… out of h-hand.

All honey

RU: Okay, listen calm down. Let's not call your therapist.

MAE: Life coach.

RU: Life coach.

MAE: She coaches me through life.

RU: Okay, just calm down.

MAE: She's my best friend. I can't breathe, I can't –

RU: Alright okay, just. Stop. Sit down.

MAE: I can't sit down, I'll die.

RU: That's ridiculous, just –

MAE: It's not ridiculous, stop calling everything ridiculous. I'll die if I sit down.

RU: Okay, fair. What do you need?

MAE: My shoes, I… I… I need to take them off, my feet are swelling.

MAE tries to kick her shoes off unsuccessfully, it turns into a stressful jig. She starts to quietly hyperventilate.

RU: Stop, okay, here, I can help you.

MAE sits in a chair while RU takes her shoes off.

RU: Better?

MAE: Yes. Can you hold them up high please?

RU: Pardon?

MAE: Elevate the shoes please, Ru, it calms me to see them up high!

RU: What?

MAE: Ru, can you hold my bloody shoes in the air please?

RU holds a shoe in each hand high above her head. MAE looking at the shoes, begins to rock from side to side and rub her chest with her right hand.

RU: Here they are, look, okay?

MAE: Okay. Yes. Okay.

RU: Okay?

RU attempts to bring the shoes down, but MAE inhales sharply so she holds them above her head. RU then starts to make the shoes do a little dance. She begins to hum a tune. As MAE is hyperventilating, she watches the shoes dance and begins to clap along to the tune.

MAE: (*Beginning to breathe normally again.*) Okay.

RU: Okay, they're coming down now.

MAE: Ah!

RU: Okay, okay. Slowly.

MAE: Thank you, Ru. I really need to box my own ears!

RU: Just maybe breathe?

MAE: (*Breathing deeply.*) Is this a bedroom?

RU: No.

MAE: Because there's no bed?

RU: Not necessarily.

MAE: Because you could put a bed in here.

RU: (*Snapping slightly.*) It's just not a bedroom.

MAE: Okay, wow.

RU: Sorry. Are you quite calm?

MAE: Yes. Forgive me. Genevieve says that panic is the enemy of the state.

RU: (*Pause.*) She really knows her stuff, that one.

MAE: She really does. I miss her.

RU: Mae, I think the best thing for you to do, right now –

All honey

MAE: Tonight?

RU: Tonight. The best thing for you to do would be to enjoy yourself.

MAE: How can I possibly?

RU: Well. Happy people are attractive. If you're smiling and thinking happy thoughts, you'll be more relaxed. And people will want to be around you.

MAE: And Barry?

RU: Sure. Barry is people so he will. Want to be around you.

MAE: So. If I pretend I'm happy. People will like me?

RU: That is what they say, isn't it?

MAE: Barry will like me?

RU: (*Reluctantly.*) Yes.

MAE: Can you show me?

RU: Sure. Just start to smile.

MAE tries to smile but is clearly upset.

RU: Well, no, not like that, that's terrifying.

MAE: Like this? (*MAE tries again.*)

RU: Yeah. Sort of. Better. Now try laughing.

RU does a laugh and MAE copies her. The first time MAE tries it sounds like she is crying. RU demonstrates again. They practice laughing for a bit.

RU: Okay, I think that's enough.

MAE: Thank you, Ru. I'm sorry I'm like this.

RU: It's fine. Really it is. It's. Not your fault.

SCENE V:
Dry Run

There is a knock on the door and LUKE sticks his head in.

LUKE: Sorry to, sorry. Ru, quick word.

RU: Of course.

MAE: Luke, of course, please come in.

LUKE: In. Without. Mae.

MAE: Oh. Oh yes. Of course. Ru. I will see you outside?

RU: I'll follow you out.

MAE: Please do. Incidentally have you seen Jessica's eyebrows? She really pushed the boat out. (*MAE leaves, with her handbag.*)

LUKE: So, I think we may have something of a mess on our hands.

RU: Right.

LUKE: Val.

RU: Did you get her a drink?

LUKE: Yeah, so she –

RU: Luke, she's not well.

LUKE: Yeah I know. So.

RU: Seriously, Luke, she is fucking insane. How do you work with her?

LUKE: Well.

RU: Didn't you tell me she tried to take legal action against someone in work she thought called her a prostitute?

LUKE: Yes, but –

RU: But then it turned out that she had just overheard a conversation where a man was telling his colleague about his prostate –

LUKE: Ru!

RU: – cancer.

LUKE: Ru.

RU: Sorry.

LUKE: Val is in the bathroom.

RU: And?

LUKE: Val has locked herself in our bathroom.

RU: Oh.

LUKE: With a bottle of gin.

RU: The gin? How did she find the gin? We didn't put the gin out.

LUKE: I hid it under the sink. She found it when she was rummaging.

RU: Why were you letting her rummage?

LUKE: I got distracted. When I looked around she was under the sink. She said she was looking for something to wash off the stench of mediocrity from this party.

RU: Right.

LUKE: Then she found the gin.

RU: Okay.

LUKE: Anyway she's locked herself in the bathroom. She seems to be muttering to herself and –

RU: Seems to be?

LUKE: Well, no, she definitely is muttering to herself. And periodically screaming, 'Give him up, he's mine'.

RU: Really? And people. Can people hear her?

LUKE: People can definitely hear her. There's no doubt in. Not a. Shadow. More than that, people. Would like to use the bathroom.

RU: Yes. Of course.

LUKE: Should I do. Something? (*Pause.*)

RU: No.

LUKE: That's probably the last thing I thought you would say.

RU: Luke. She's been with Barry.

LUKE: Who? Val?

RU: Yes, Val. It's Barry.

LUKE: Bollox.

RU: She is. She has been. With. Barry. Mae thinks Barry has been, is being with someone else. She found a nightgown.

LUKE: You said that was for his mother.

RU: Yes, but then Val mentioned that she had a nightgown. And that it was saucy.

LUKE: Ah, come on. What does that even mean?

RU: She asked about Barry. She asked how Barry and I were. I told her I was with Luke and she said that's what I said and I said no you said Barry and then she lost her mind trying to correct me.

LUKE: She mentioned Barry's name and she has a nightgown.

RU: A saucy nightgown.

LUKE: A saucy nightgown. That's your evidence?

RU: Yes. (*Pause.*) And and then she said baby.

LUKE: Baby?

RU: Barry always says baby, Mae says it now. And Val does too.

LUKE: Okay, just breathe, sweet. Potato. Face.

RU: Luke, eat something!

LUKE: Yeah, okay.

RU: Luke, he is the worst kind of person.

All honey

LUKE: He is. He really is, but let's just –

RU: No! Oh Barry, I'm Barry, I try to sleep with everything. Barry. We've all slept with Barry. Oh we've all slept with Barry. Well, I haven't slept with Barry because he's a prick. But Barry's tried. Luke, he's done this to Mae so. Many. Times.

LUKE: Okay, alright. That's enough. Okay. I think we should stop talking about Barry. He's not even here. Let's just get Val out of the bathroom and keep Mae away from the balcony.

RU: I hate him, Luke.

LUKE: I know.

BARRY sticks his head around the door.

BARRY: Who do you hate?

LUKE: Barry.

RU: Barry.

BARRY: (*Joyfully.*) Barry!

LUKE: Hi. Barry.

BARRY: Hello, ladies and gents, happy house warming. I brought you a special spoon. (*BARRY hands RU a large ladle with tags on it. It is wrapped in several brightly coloured ribbons that only cover a portion of it.*)

LUKE: Thanks, Barry. Ru loves soup.

RU: No, I don't.

LUKE: What are you doing? Have you been inside?

BARRY: No, not yet. I met Jessica across the road, she was going to the bathroom in Finnegan's. Said yours was ocupado. Hey, what's wrong with her face?

RU: Nothing.

LUKE: Ru, would you like a drink? You haven't had a chance to. Sit down. And. Drink.

RU: Actually, Luke, I would like a word with Ba –

LUKE: No, why don't you go on out and get a drink and chat with Mae? We'll be out right after you.

BARRY: Mae's here already?

RU: Yes.

BARRY: Fine.

LUKE: Great.

BARRY: Good.

RU: (*Pause.*) I'll go grab a drink and Mae and trot right back in here, shall I?

LUKE: No.

BARRY: What?

LUKE: No.

BARRY: Why?

RU: Why not? How was your emergency, Barry?

BARRY: It was. Emergent.

LUKE: (*Quietly.*) Nope.

RU: I hope it was important.

BARRY: It was. It really was.

LUKE: Ru.

RU: Luke, can I speak to you outside for a second please? (*Pause.*)

LUKE: Yeah. Sure.

RU leaves and LUKE slowly follows her. BARRY stares at the door for a moment. He then moves towards the mirror.

BARRY: Hey, I'm Barry. Barry, yeah. I'm Barry. Bar. Bar Bar. Like the elephant, exactly. So where are you from? Kewl kewl, I don't where that is (*Laughs.*) Yeah, I'm from Dalkey, my mum is a solicitor. No. Yeah no. Actually. I'm a solicitor. A big one. A big solicitor. I'm the biggest solicitor. If you pick up what I am putting down –

LUKE comes back in the room quickly, still holding the spoon.

SCENE VI:
She's Here

BARRY: So.

LUKE: Hi.

BARRY: Nicely done.

LUKE: Yeah.

BARRY: Not really, though. That was very clumsy.

LUKE: Yeah. (*Pause. LUKE does not make eye contact with BARRY.*)

BARRY: What's wrong?

LUKE: Ru knows. (*Pause.*)

BARRY: She what?

LUKE: She knows.

Pause. Next lines are spoken simultaneously.

BARRY: How the fuck did she find out? What did you say to her, are you out of your head, why hasn't she tried to murder me yet? Is she going to tell about us? Because, according to you, it was nothing. Nothing.

LUKE: Not about that, about you and your. What the fuck do you think I'd tell her that for, it wasn't even, nothing. It was nothing. I'm out of my mind? It wasn't even anything. It was nothing.

Pause.

BARRY: What?

LUKE: What?

BARRY: What does she know?

LUKE: About Val. You fuck.

BARRY: Oh Jesus. Val? You nearly. I mean. Christ. Wow. Crisis averted.

BARRY holds up his hand in a celebratory fashion, physically imploring LUKE for a high five or a fist pump or something of that manner. LUKE does not respond.

LUKE: My girlfriend knows you're... (*gesturing*) with a mental person behind her best friend's back. How is that. Crisis averted?

BARRY: Yes but. From where I was standing. I thought your girlfriend knew –

LUKE: No, she doesn't.

BARRY: Great. We can keep pretending it never happened.

LUKE: I'm not pretending, I just don't want to talk about –

BARRY: Fine, yeah, great, grand. How does Ru know about Val?

LUKE: She doesn't, well. She put it together. Have you gotten rid of Val? How did it go?

BARRY: Yeah, not bad. She put it together?

LUKE: What do you mean not bad?

BARRY: Well.

LUKE: Yes?

BARRY: Yeah. Well. It went fine for me. She was driving, dropping me home. I asked her to pull into a garage. Told her I needed some. Pop. Asked did she want anything. No. Asked could I have her car keys for the loyalty card. Yeah. Took the car keys. Locked the car from the outside. Then I shouted. 'It's over. You're mental. I hate you.' Threw the keys as far away as I could. Then ran all the way home.

LUKE: Right.

BARRY: Mmm. So from my perspective. Not bad.

LUKE: Bit of exercise.

BARRY: Exactly, yeah. So, sorry, how does Ru know about Val?

LUKE: She doesn't know, she pieced it together. But her evidence is bullshit.

All honey

BARRY: Oh yeah? What does she have?

LUKE: Well, Mae thinks you're... (*Gesturing.*)

BARRY: Doing sex on –

LUKE: Barry, please. She thinks you're having. Intercourse. With someone. Else. And she told Ru.

BARRY: Does she actually?

LUKE: Yes.

BARRY: I can't believe she'd think that.

LUKE: You have been with someone else. Did you not think she'd eventually realise?

BARRY: She's never copped before. She's smart as anything but not too bright if you know what I mean.

LUKE: No. I don't know what you mean.

BARRY: Well, she's not supposed to know.

LUKE: I wish I didn't know. I hate knowing. I can't lie. Don't ever tell me again. Or just break up with Mae.

BARRY: How does Mae know?

LUKE: She said something about a nightgown.

BARRY: That fucking nightgown.

LUKE: Was it for your mother?

BARRY: No.

LUKE: It was for Val?

BARRY: (*Nodding.*) The psychotic.

LUKE: Go way.

BARRY: Yeah. She fucking loves nightgowns.

LUKE: Jesus, fair play to Ru.

BARRY: Did she guess that?

LUKE: Yeah.

BARRY: Jesus, yeah, fair play to her.

LUKE: It was the nightgown, the fact that you used to work with Val, and something about the way you say baby the whole time.

BARRY: I never say baby.

LUKE: You do.

BARRY: I do not.

LUKE: Ah, you do.

BARRY: Nope. Bullshit evidence.

LUKE: Oh, utter shite. She's right though.

BARRY: She is that.

LUKE: Listen, I've to go deal with that em. Bathroom situation. Can you. Stay here?

BARRY: Right. Wow. Okay.

LUKE: Yeah. Do you mind?

BARRY: Well, I'd prefer not to.

LUKE: I know, I know, I just need you to stay here and. Unwrap this spoon. (*LUKE proffers the spoon to BARRY. Pause.*)

BARRY: Now? (*BARRY takes the spoon.*)

LUKE: Yep, Ru will want to use it almost immediately.

BARRY: She really does like soup, huh?

LUKE: She really does.

BARRY: Amazing gift, Barry.

LUKE: Exactly. So if you could just do that, I'll be back in a second and we can go get a drink.

BARRY: Okay. (*LUKE goes to leave again.*) Luke?

LUKE: Yeah?

BARRY: Would Ru tell Mae? About Val?

LUKE: No. I don't think so. She wouldn't want to upset Mae.

BARRY: No. Yeah. (*LUKE goes to leave.*)

BARRY: I will. Make a clean breast of it.

LUKE: You should. I just hope Ru doesn't run into Val again, otherwise Mae might finish with you tonight.

BARRY: (*Laughing.*) Yeah. (*LUKE leaves.*) Wait what.

BARRY stands still thinking for a moment then begins removing the ribbons and/or cellotape from the spoon. The door silently opens and VAL slinks in wearing a cow mask. She shuts the door and BARRY realises he is not alone in the room. He looks up, but not at VAL.

BARRY: (*Whispering.*) Oh God.

VAL reopens the door behind her and acts like she just came in the room. BARRY spins around.

VAL: (*Laughing at the door.*) Oh, that's so funny. Back in a tick, Tiernach. (*She closes the door behind her.*) Oh. Hello. I was actually having a conversation with my new friends here. Who are him? He's new –

BARRY: What are you doing here?

VAL: I was invited.

BARRY: Val –

VAL: Ah. So you haven't forgotten me? Can't get me over, off your mind. Can't get my name off your lips, hmm?

BARRY: Yeah. Heeey, Val. Are you. How are. You look. Did you get home okay last night?

VAL: I got home fine, yes, thank you. A man found… fetched my keys. I didn't even ask him to.

BARRY: That is super.

VAL: So I see you're lurking in the box room, obviously to catch me for a quiet word. Typical. Well, I'm busy.

BARRY: I honestly didn't know you were here. (*VAL looks at BARRY for a moment.*)

VAL: That was some fun last night, wasn't it?

BARRY: Eh, well it was. A different sort of –

VAL: Of?

BARRY: Game?

VAL: Game?

BARRY: Look, Val, I think I might pop off.

VAL: Please. Do you think I'm simple? You don't want to. Pop off. You think you can just swan in to this soirée and bend down on your bent knee and offer me some moon? You have another thing coming to you, Sally. Who do you think you are? Some kind of superstar?

BARRY: What?

VAL: What do you think?

BARRY: Val. I think we should. Not communicate. Ever. Never.

VAL: What?

BARRY: I. Would just like it if we were not in contact.

VAL: And I will not respond to threats or pleas or sandwiches. I. Like. Sushi.

BARRY: I'm sorry?

VAL: I put diamonds in my sushi. That is me.

BARRY: Yeah, Val, I think I might leave you to it. (*BARRY makes for the door.*)

VAL: (*Raising her voice.*) You lied to me. (*BARRY stops moving.*) You lied to me. You liked to me, so many times. You you said you were finished

All honey

with Mae. Lie. You said you were allergic to dust. False, lie. Never even saw an inhaler. You said you wanted to get pop. LIE. You said that you love me. LIE. Why do you lie all the time?

BARRY: I'm sorry.

VAL: No. No, no sorry. Why? Why? It's not me. I'm. Really lovely. It must be you.

BARRY: I don't know.

VAL: Does it make you feel good?

BARRY: Yes.

VAL: Well, it makes everyone else feel like dirt.

BARRY: (*Pause.*) I don't know what to say.

VAL: Don't say anything. (*Pause.*) Don't say anything. It will do no good. You cannot win me back.

BARRY: Well, I don't actually –

VAL: You will never win me over again. I don't care how much you love me.

BARRY: Oh. How awful. What a punishment.

VAL: Or maybe I could just tell Mae everything? It would be the perfect reason to eject you from her house.

BARRY: Well, no, don't. Do that. It's hard enough losing you.

VAL: Well, maybe I won't have to tell Mae. I could just show her the pictures of your genitals I have on my hand-held telephone with a camera.

BARRY: Look, Val, please don't. I'm talking to her tomorrow, we'll be finished. I promise.

VAL: Tomorrow? She's here now! I'll get her. Mae!

LUKE sticks his head in the door.

LUKE: Hey we're all clear – no we're not.

VAL: Hi Luke. Where's Mae?

LUKE: Mae? Mae is actually gone.

VAL: No, she's not.

LUKE: She is.

BARRY: Is she?

LUKE: Yes. Ru and Mae went to buy more gin. We ran out.

VAL: No problems. I'll wait outside for them. With. My. Phone.

VAL leaves.

SCENE VII:
Semantics

LUKE: I'm sorry, Barry, I thought she was.

BARRY: So. She's here.

LUKE: Yeah. She's here.

BARRY: She's here.

LUKE: Yeah.

BARRY: She's here. Why is she here?

LUKE: I –

BARRY: Where's Mae?

LUKE: They actually have gone to buy more gin. I asked Ru to take Mae.

BARRY: How long do we have?

LUKE: Like five minutes?

BARRY: I told you.

LUKE: I know. You told me. I know you told me –

BARRY: Well, I told you I never wanted to see her again.

LUKE: I know. I didn't invite her. I don't know why she's here.

BARRY: (*Getting irritated.*) Yeah, but she is here.

LUKE: I know she's here. I didn't invite her. (*Pause.*) And why should I have to keep her away?

BARRY: Jesus, don't.

LUKE: No, why am I trying to keep your side pieces –

BARRY: Side pieces, for fuck sake, cop on will you, we're not Americans.

LUKE: Why am I preventing your women from coming to my house, where my girlfriend –

BARRY: Luke, it's an apartment.

LUKE: My home, where my girlfriend –

BARRY: (*Sneering.*) Your girlfriend.

LUKE: Yes. My, my girlfriend. Yeah, she is mine.

BARRY: Yeah, but come on, bit hypocritical, Luke –

LUKE: Look. I tried to stop her. I couldn't stop her. The lads brought her. She's here.

BARRY: Yeah, she is here. And now I have to leave with my girlfriend because Val is a liability.

LUKE: She wouldn't have been as much of a liability if you hadn't –

BARRY: Ah, she would.

LUKE: And is Mae still your girlfriend? Because you told me you moved out. Is she your fucking girlfriend still?

BARRY: Look. This has all gotten. A bit. What do you care who I'm with? I mean we're not –

LUKE: I don't care. No we're not. Anything. We're not anything.

BARRY: Are we not?

LUKE: Look, it was one. I was in a bad place.

BARRY: It was last week.

LUKE: It was just one.

BARRY: It was one what?

LUKE: (*Pause.*) Slip.

BARRY: You're right, we're not anything. So why are you getting upset when all my chickens come home goosed?

LUKE: What?

BARRY: What?

LUKE: Come home what?

BARRY: Goosed.

LUKE: That's not it.

BARRY: What?

LUKE: That's not the phrase.

BARRY: Yes, it is.

LUKE: When all your chickens come home goosed?

BARRY: Yeah.

LUKE: What like. Locked chickens?

BARRY: Yeah.

LUKE: (*Smiling.*) That's not the phrase.

BARRY: No, listen. Semantics.

LUKE: You don't know what semantics means.

BARRY: I don't see how that's relevant. (*Pause.*) We have fun.

LUKE: Shut the fuck up.

BARRY: What's this? Why are you so upset?

LUKE: I'm not.

BARRY: You are. Why do you care?

LUKE: (*Quietly.*) I don't care.

BARRY: You don't care? Because you look like you care. (*Pause.*) You look like you fucking care.

LUKE: (*Getting louder.*) No, I don't fucking. Look. I tried to. I told them not to bring her. I'm sorry she's here. I… I don't even know what you were doing with her, she's fucking mental.

BARRY: I know she's mental, she's fucking crazy, but she's kinda sexy and I can't. Help. It. I mean, she wanted me.

LUKE: Oh for –

BARRY: Stop now, she went for me. She stood in front of me in the elevator, when it was just the two of us and put her arse on my.

LUKE: Don't.

BARRY: I mean. What could I do? I was solid as a rock.

LUKE: Don't.

BARRY: Before I knew what was happening the lad was out and I was absolutely drilling into her arse –

LUKE: Ah, Barry, I asked you not to.

BARRY: What was I supposed to do?

LUKE: What were you supposed to do? Tell her to stop? Tell her you live with your girlfriend. Don't take your penis out. There. There's at least three things you could have done.

BARRY: Why does it matter to you? You would have done it too.

LUKE: That is bollox. I wouldn't do that – (*Barry coming in on top of Luke (verbally.)*)

BARRY: (*Mockingly.*) You wouldn't do that –

LUKE: No. I wouldn't do what you did. Do you not feel guilty?

BARRY: (*Pause.*) No.

LUKE: That's impossible.

BARRY: I don't.

LUKE: I don't believe that because I can't fucking sleep. (*Pause.*)

BARRY: Sorry.

LUKE: What is wrong with you?

BARRY: I don't know.

LUKE: Do you not feel anything?

BARRY: No.

LUKE: Nothing?

BARRY: I don't feel anything. (*Pause. LUKE stares at BARRY. BARRY moves close to LUKE.*) I kissed a stranger on the dance floor of a bar while Mae was getting us drinks. I had sex with someone in her house while she was upstairs in bed. I'm in here with you. And. Nothing.

LUKE: I can't get it out of my head.

B*ARRY kisses LUKE. The door opens silently. LUKE pushes BARRY away. VAL is standing in the doorway. They hear her.*

VAL: Fuck off.

SCENE VIII:
Theatrics

BARRY: Val.

LUKE: Fuck.

VAL: Fuck Val is right –

LUKE: I thought you –

VAL: What the fuck is this boys? (*Silence.*) What the fuck is this?

All honey

LUKE: It's.

BARRY: We're.

LUKE: It's.

BARRY: Practice. (*Silence.*)

VAL: Practice?

LUKE: Yep.

BARRY: Mmhmm.

LUKE: Rehearsals.

VAL: Is it?

LUKE: It is.

BARRY: Yes. Just practising.

LUKE: Rehearsing.

BARRY: Rehearsing.

VAL: For?

LUKE and BARRY make a 'thinking' noise and look at each other.

LUKE: A play?

VAL: A play?

BARRY: No –

LUKE: No, listen –

BARRY: No, it is –

LUKE: We joined an am dram society for a little bit of confidence and –

BARRY: And we were cast in a famous play.

LUKE: A very famous play.

VAL: (*Pause.*) What's it called? Quickly!

BARRY: Ahhhh –

LUKE: Ehh –

BARRY: Hot? Hot –

LUKE: Chair.

BARRY: (*Under his breath.*) For fuck sake.

VAL: (*Pause.*) *Hot Hot Chair*?

LUKE: Just *Hot Chair*.

BARRY: (*Under his breath.*) That's not better.

VAL: I can hear you.

LUKE: It's a new play.

VAL: The very famous, new play, *Hot Chair*?.

BARRY: That's the one.

LUKE: Yep.

VAL: (*Pause.*) Okay. Do a bit.

BARRY: From?

VAL: The play. Do a bit from the play.

BARRY: It's really not ready.

LUKE: We haven't warmed up.

VAL: Okay. (*VAL moves towards the door. The boys jump.*)

BARRY: No! No. Luke? Start the play.

LUKE: Okay fine, fine. (*Clears his throat.*) What are you doing, Mordecai?

BARRY: Jesus. I'm. Harvesting the chairs.

LUKE: Taking them in from the sun?

BARRY: That's right. The townspeople will never want to buy. Hot chairs.

LUKE: Skip to the end.

BARRY: When the farm was gone. Tiernach and Mordecai realised they were –

LUKE: Best friends. And so they sealed their friendship with a kiss. (*BARRY and LUKE lean in and do a fake kiss.*)

BARRY: And in that moment they knew. They were all hot chairs.

Pause. They look at VAL. Pause.

LUKE: Val please –

VAL: Is this the face of a fool?

BARRY: No.

LUKE: God, no.

VAL: No, it is not.

BARRY: Val –

VAL: Quelle surprise, Barry… but you, Luke. This is quite the quelle surprise.

LUKE: What?

VAL: I expected this from him. He's a monster. I thought you were nice.

LUKE: Val. You're imagining things. This isn't at all what you think.

BARRY: It really was practice.

VAL: Shut up, Barry. When did it first happen, Luke? Recently? Barry loves theatrics. Had you signed the lease yet? You are something. Ru is going to be devastated.

LUKE: Val, please please don't say anything. This was nothing.

VAL: Oh I have to say something, Luke, she's my best friend. Did you really think I was going to keep this from her? How could I look her in the eye knowing what I now know?

LUKE: Your best friend?

BARRY: Easy, Luke. Val, I really need to talk to you alone.

VAL: No.

BARRY: Val, please. (*Pause.*) I miss you.

VAL: The last time you saw me you said you didn't think we should communicate, ever never.

BARRY: Yes, I know, but the time apart made me realise… I need to speak with you alone. Maybe outside this apartment? Far away.

VAL: No. I don't want to be alone with you, Barry. Not with all this information I just gleaned. All this explosive information. I'm going outside this instant to tell a stranger what you've been doing so you two don't try to murder me.

LUKE: We're not going to murder you, Val, just hang –

VAL: Just hang on a second till we murder you, I know your game.

BARRY: Val, I actually definitely still love you.

VAL: Come off it, Barry, I've seen the movies.

LUKE: Val, please God don't tell anyone. It was a mistake.

BARRY: I think we could still be together.

VAL: No, Barry, see that would never work because I wouldn't pay your rent. (*Buzzer sounds.*) Oh that must be the girls, let's go do this in front of everyone, shall we?

VAL flings opens the door and turns left. The boys look at each other then follow her, leaving the door open.

SCENE IX:
She Could Be A Prostitute

A few moments later RU and MAE walk past the door, coming from the right with a bottle of gin and an open bottle of wine. RU sees the door open and walks in the room. MAE follows her, closing the door behind them. MAE is still carrying her handbag.

All honey

MAE: About 33 million.

RU: Fuck off. How did you work that out?

MAE: Apparently on average, people spend 0.45% of their lives doing intercourse. So if there's 7.4 thousand million people on earth, multiply by .0045, that's about 33 million.

RU: Are having sex right now?

MAE: Yes. Well. That figure includes children.

RU: Oh.

MAE: I'd need to know the statistic of people the legal age.

RU: How did you do that so quickly?

MAE: It's really simple maths, Ru.

RU: Is it?

MAE: Genevieve is wonderful at maths.

RU: Jesus.

MAE: She just understands me.

RU: Yeah, well, I mean, you pay her.

MAE: Don't make it sound so dirty. She's not a prostitute.

RU: No, sorry, I wasn't implying that at all –

MAE: Don't get me wrong, she could be.

RU: What?

MAE: Genevieve. She could be a prostitute.

RU: Could she?

MAE: Of the highest class though, because she's very beautiful.

RU: Oh. Yeah.

MAE: I don't even think you could call her a prostitute, she's far too classy.

RU: Mmm.

MAE: No one would be able to afford her!

RU: She'd be very expensive?

MAE: I could probably afford her.

RU: (*Pause.*) How often do you see Genevieve?

MAE: Oh, sort of once every… 42 hours.

RU: That is a lot of life coaching sessions.

MAE: Yes, well, I need a lot of life coaching.

RU: Do you? Are they all in her office?

MAE: No, gosh no, lives aren't spent in offices, Ru. That's what Genevieve says.

RU: You work in an office.

MAE: Yes, but life…

RU: You practically live in your office.

MAE: Yes, but I have a life, Ru.

RU: So where do you meet Genevieve?

MAE: She has a darling little cottage by the canal, we go there most evenings.

RU: And what do you do in your sessions?

MAE: Mainly laugh.

RU: And?

MAE: Oh, how we laugh.

RU: What else though?

MAE: Well, Genevieve has cleverly themed our sessions. We have a cheese session, a wine session, a cheese and wine session and also hug therapy.

All honey

RU: I have so many questions but I'll just start with… hug therapy?

MAE: Oh, it's incredible, we lie on her couch and just hold each other for hours.

RU: Right.

MAE: Mmm.

RU: Mae, would it be so bad. If Barry were to. Not be around anymore.

MAE: Oh. But I love Barry.

RU: Why?

MAE: Well. You don't know what he's like when we're alone.

RU: What does Genevieve think of Barry?

MAE: She says I have to come to that decision on my own. She doesn't want me to resent her. Which is mental because she's literally perfect.

RU: Mae. Does Barry make you feel as good as say, Genevieve does?

MAE: No one makes me feel as good as Genevieve does, Ru, but you can't be in love with your life coach!

RU: Can you not?

The door flies open and in walks VAL followed by LUKE.

VAL: Ladies!

RU: Val.

MAE: Hello.

LUKE. Ru, don't –

VAL: Now, Luke. Don't spoil the surprise!

MAE: What's your name?

VAL: I'm Val, I'm –

LUKE: A prostitute.

RU: Luke?

VAL: I'm Val and I'm not a prostitute, even though I could be. (*As VAL is introducing herself to MAE, BARRY comes into the room.*)

BARRY: Luke, where the fuck did she? Heeeeeeey. Girls.

LUKE: Everyone's here, Barry.

RU: Barry.

MAE: Barry!

VAL: Prick.

BARRY: Barry.

RU: Well, I wasn't going to. But since we have a bit of privacy. Mae. Barry has something to tell you.

BARRY: No, I don't.

RU: Barry.

BARRY: No, Ru.

RU: Fine. Coward. I'll do it.

VAL: I'll take it from here, Ru.

RU: What?

LUKE: Val. Ru was speaking. Please don't –

RU: Don't what? (*VAL takes MAE by the hand.*)

VAL: Mae, I think we could be friends. Really good friends. Even better friends than Ru and I.

MAE: That's nice.

RU: We're not friends.

VAL: Ru, please, I'm speaking. But, Mae, I have to tell you something about Barry. This isn't going to be easy to hear but just know that you have the most wonderful hair that I have ever seen.

RU: Okay, no, Mae –

All honey

VAL: Fine, Ru, I was trying to deliver the bad news with some finesse but here, I'll just throw it at her like a raw steak. Mae, Barry has been sleeping with Luke.

RU: (*Silence.*) You are unbelievable, that's ridiculous. (*Silence.*) Luke? Isn't she unbelievable?

VAL: I saw them kissing in here. Tonight.

MAE: You were with Luke?

RU: No, he wasn't.

MAE: Were you?

RU: Luke?

BARRY: We were locked, Mae, it was only once.

MAE: Once? Luke?

VAL: Twice, they kissed tonight.

LUKE: And, Val, Barry was with Val for ages.

MAE: Luke?

VAL: Don't be so dramatic, Luke, it was 27 weeks. Max. And I don't even like him, Mae.

MAE: (*Silence.*) Of course you were.

BARRY: Mae –

MAE: No. Don't.

BARRY: I know.

MAE: No really. This time. Just don't.

BARRY: Okay.

MAE: Did you think I wouldn't find out?

BARRY: I don't know what I thought. I'm sorry for hurting –

MAE: Barry, do you have any idea –

BARRY: I know –

MAE: No, you don't. I stood up for you.

BARRY: But I don't deserve it.

MAE: I know that. I don't know why I did it.

BARRY: (*Pause.*) You're not really in love with me, Mae. You just. Think you should be.

MAE: Please don't give me advice, Barry. I have Genevieve for that.

BARRY: Yeah, I know.

MAE: Your things will be in the garden tomorrow. Don't contact me again.

BARRY: Jesus, Mae, let's not lose our heads here, I can stay until next week, can't I?

MAE: No, you cannot. I need to see Genevieve.

BARRY: Mae –

MAE: Barry, just leave it. I'm sorry, Ru, I have to go.

VAL: Mae, perhaps I can accompany you outside and we could grab a drink? And then we can continue this friendship the way we've always wanted to.

MAE: I can't remember your name.

VAL: Excellent. Gentlemen. Ru.

MAE leaves the room and VAL trots out after her.

BARRY: Fuck.

LUKE: Ru? (*Silence*) Ru? (*Silence.*) Ru, please say something.

RU: You wanted to move in.

LUKE: Ru, I'm so sorry.

RU: You wanted to move in. You asked me. You let me sign the lease. You signed the lease. Why did you sign the lease.

LUKE: I didn't know, I –

RU: Why did you sign the lease?

LUKE: I wanted to live with you.

RU: Then why did you fuck Barry?

LUKE: I don't. Know.

RU: So you did.

LUKE: I don't –

RU: Are you gay?

LUKE: No, I'm not. I was. So drunk and. I don't know. I've never felt like that before. I don't feel like that now.

RU: But you were just going to carry on hanging out with him?

LUKE: I didn't know what to do, he's the only one I could talk to.

RU: Is he?

Silence.

LUKE: I didn't mean that.

RU: Get out.

LUKE: Ru, please.

RU: Luke, get out.

LUKE: Ru, please. Don't make. Let's talk. I haven't been talking to you, I swear I can explain.

RU: Get the fuck out, Luke. I don't want to look at you. (*Pause.*) Close the door (*LUKE leaves and closes the door after him. Silence. BARRY looks around the room. He makes a loud noise as if to say 'glad that's all over'.*)

BARRY: Ahhhh. That was. Weird. (*RU is fixed on the door/wall. Staring anywhere except at BARRY*) You alright, Ru? (*RU still fixed. Silence.*) I think I'll just –

RU: Fuck off, Barry.

RU leaves.

THE END

Normal

Caitríona Daly

First produced at the Dublin Fringe Festival in The Lir Academy in September 2017. Subsequently transferred to Bewleys Café Theatre in April 2018 where the cast and crew were as follows:

Director: Maisie Lee
Designer: Shane Gill
Producer: Denis Horan

Characters & Cast:

HELEN (*Aged 27*): Caoimhe O'Malley
PHIL (*Aged 50*) : Karen Ardiff

—

Caitríona Daly is a playwright from Dublin. She is a graduate from The Lir Academy and the Royal Court's Young Playwrights Programme and an alumnus of the Irish Theatre Institute's Six in the Attic initiative. Her plays have been produced both nationally and internationally. She was nominated for the Fishamble New Writing Award in 2017 and an Irish Times Theatre Award for Best New Play in 2016. She is currently under commission with Fishamble: The New Play Company.

Dublin, present day. A pub function room, the floor is covered in crisps, biscuits, confetti and semi-deflated balloons. It looks like a 'party bomb' has hit it. HELEN is sitting with her head in her hands. PHIL enters, slamming the door behind her. Helen jumps up and resumes cleaning. Unless otherwise instructed, it is assumed that the actors are cleaning the set throughout most of the play.

> *(–) denotes being cut off.*
>
> *(…) denotes a hesitant beat.*
>
> *(\) denotes an overlapping of dialogue.*

PHIL: He's in the car.

HELEN avoids her and keeps cleaning. PHIL stalks around her in an attempt to make eye contact.

PHIL: I said he's in the car; we got him in the car. (*Pause.*)

HELEN: (*While cleaning.*) Good. (*Pause.*)

PHIL: Good? Good.

PHIL rolls her sleeves up and unrolls a black sack. HELEN still ignoring her goes on cleaning. A glass smashes.

HELEN: I'll get it.

HELEN sweeps it up. PHIL emerges from a cupboard with a dustpan.

HELEN: I said I have it, Phil. (*PHIL uses the dustpan where HELEN just swept. HELEN groans. Silence.*) It, eh, doesn't look like anyone liked the cakes. (*Pause.*) Or maybe, I just bought too many... Probably did to be honest, my eyes are always bigger than my belly... and my wallet too, unfortunately... Did you try the cakes, Phil?

PHIL: No.

HELEN: Oh, they were nice, the cakes. I bought them in Marks and Spencer's.

PHIL: Very expensive.

HELEN: Worth it though, for Gary, for a birthday.

PHIL: Too much cream.

HELEN: A bit of cream never hurt anyone too much... I think.

PHIL: Bad for your gallbladder. Humans can't process dairy, not like that.

HELEN: Really? I've never heard that before. I'll stay away from the Ben and Jerry's so. (*Beat.*) Seems a shame to be throwing them out all the same.

PHIL: Waste of money alright... (*Beat.*) How much did Marks and Spencer's steal from you for those, Helen?

HELEN: I can't remember. Mustn't have been too much though, I'd've remembered if I'd had to re-mortgage the house.

PHIL: You bought a house?

HELEN: No, I... A joke. It was a joke.

PHIL: You're too young to buy a house.

HELEN: I know. It was a joke. (*Beat.*) Mind you, house prices in Dublin at the moment, now that's a joke.

PHIL: You've been looking then?

HELEN: No. (*Beat.*) You just hear about it... that's all. In the newspapers and... stuff.

PHIL: Hmmm.

HELEN: (*Silence.*) Fake news maybe… heh… I wish.

PHIL: That's Dublin for you I suppose, ripping everyone off, as usual. (*Beat.*) You're from Dublin, aren't you, Helen?

HELEN: Yes.

PHIL: Awful place, I never got used to it.

HELEN: Where are you from, Phil?

PHIL: Kildare

HELEN: Really? You'd never know your accent, it's… Kildare is not too far though, at least.

PHIL: It feels like it. Feels like a far cry from Dublin most of the time.

HELEN: (*Beat.*) It's nice though, Kildare.

PHIL: Have you been?

HELEN: Just once.

PHIL: Where?

HELEN: Punchestown

PHIL: For the races?

HELEN: Oxegen

PHIL: Yes, well, that'd hardly be Kildare for you now. (*A balloon pops.*)

HELEN: Still though, nice, very green. (*Another balloon pops.*)

PHIL: I suppose the balloons are from Marks and Spencer's too? How much do balloons cost in Marks and Spencer's? I'd say you'd be lucky getting change of a tenner for balloons from Marks and Sparks.

HELEN: Two Euro World. They were two euro in Two Euro World, the balloons.

PHIL: Oh… explains the popping so.

HELEN: Maybe, yeah.

PHIL: (*Beat.*) Awful place, Two Euro World, teeming with people, how are you expected to shop if you can't see anything with the people bustling around the place and I don't care what anyone says, I don't trust anything that's that cheap.

HELEN: Handy though, if you're on a budget.

PHIL: I'm not on a budget.

HELEN: I wasn't saying you were, just if you are, it's handy.

PHIL: For things like balloons, maybe. But anyone who's cracked enough to buy the food on their table there needs to have their head checked. I mean if food could be that cheap, wouldn't it be? I mean where did it come from? It hardly fell from the sky. The expiration dates or something, it all must be gone off. Lily bought her eggs there once and she said never again. (*Begins rummaging in a black sack.*) Fluff and green specks on them, half cracked. I don't care how appealing a dozen eggs for two euro is, there's something not right with that. (*Beat.*) Have you met Lily? My sister, Gary's aunt, I'm surprised she wasn't here tonight.

HELEN: I've never met her.

PHIL: Haven't you? She's always around the house. It's a shame, I'm sure she'd be sad to have missed it, your party. Or maybe not given the... mess.

HELEN: I knew Gary had an aunt, you had a sister. I just, I didn't realise you were so close.

PHIL: Oh yeah, she's been a huge part of Gary's life alright. My right hand woman is Lily. She lives alone, she's lonely, so in a way Gary is as much a help to her as she to him. Not to belittle how much she helps him because she does and it's an awful shame that she's not here tonight.

HELEN: I asked Gary who he... he didn't say, I didn't know, I'm sorry, Phil.

PHIL: Yes, well, I'd say 'next time' but we know that that's not going to happen.

HELEN: That's a little premature.

PHIL: It was premature when you suggested having a party in the first place.

HELEN: That's not fair, there were good bits... tonight.

PHIL: Really? Which was your favourite? When he stood on your hand or when he tried to rip the fixtures off the wall?

HELEN: That's not fair.

PHIL: No, it's not. It's not fair.

HELEN: (*On cutting herself with glass.*) Fuck!

PHIL: Excuse me!

HELEN: There's just some... there's some glass in the bag.

PHIL: I told you. Are you bleeding?

HELEN: Just a trickle.

PHIL: We'll need bandages so... (*PHIL starts searching.*)

HELEN: No, I'm fine! (*Beat.*) There! 20th of November!

PHIL: What?

HELEN: The biscuits, I got them in Two Euro World, the expiration date is fine.

PHIL: Must have fallen off the back of a van so. Give me your finger.

HELEN: I'm fine, it's fine.

PHIL: Fine.

HELEN: (*Beat.*) Do you want one?

PHIL: No. (*HELEN eats a biscuit*) A bit of antiseptic wouldn't go a miss. Wouldn't know what's on these floors.

HELEN: (*Beat.*) Julie's left her cardigan.

PHIL: Who?

HELEN: Julie, my friend, long blonde hair, her boyfriend is Tom.

PHIL: I've never met them.

HELEN: Well, they were here tonight so you could've met them, if you had talked to anyone.

PHIL: Oh, I'm so sorry I didn't talk to anyone. I was too busy trying to mind my son in your sensory palace here.

HELEN: Well, they're nice. You would have liked them.

PHIL: They ran out of here soon enough, probably didn't have a second thought for their belongings. You can't blame June for leaving her jumper.

HELEN: It's Julie and it's her cardigan.

PHIL: I hope they had somewhere to move on to, Julie and the others? When the party was cut short? They seemed fond of a party so hopefully they had another one to crash. Must have been annoyed having this one end so soon.

HELEN: No they understood the situation and were happy enough to move on when the time came.

PHIL: Understood? You've spoken to them about Gary, so, have you?

HELEN: I haven't needed to, Phil. They're 'our' friends, mine and Gary's, we see them all the time.

PHIL: This happens all the time?

HELEN: Of course it doesn't…

PHIL: I hardly see them hanging around much longer if incidents like tonight keep happening. They'll get fed up, tired, if history has taught me anything, it's that.

HELEN: They understand.

PHIL: Oh they understand alright, I saw them.

HELEN: Stop it, Phil.

PHIL: For God's sake, Helen. Wake up.

HELEN: They didn't run out of here, Phil. They didn't cut their night short and they're not tired and they're not fed up okay? They know and love Gary, they understood what was going on and were more than willing to help in any way they could. You saw… you saw, Phil! I had to stop Michael from ringing an ambulance but he wanted to do it, he would have gone with Gary if he needed to, they're our friends.

PHIL: I've never met them.

HELEN: Do you think Gary has no friends?

PHIL: I've never met them.

HELEN: No life, no? He has no life, Phil, is that what you think?

PHIL: Oh you've made perfectly sure, Helen, that Gary has whatever idea of a life it is you have yourself. God knows the rest of us aren't good enough for you, or him, apparently.

HELEN: Well, I'm sorry you feel that way. And I'm sorry you've never met our friends before, that they're not your Facebook friends, but next time we "hit the club" I'll be sure to invite you.

PHIL: "Hit the club??" What is wrong with you? (*Pause.*)

HELEN: I'm I, I'm messing I don't even like clubbing. We don't go clubbing, Phil. Me and Gary, our friends, we don't do that. We just go for tea really, meals, the odd drink in a pub.

PHIL: Oh yes, the odd drink in a pub and the odd desertion in town.

HELEN: How many times… We talked about that… You're either going to get over it or…

PHIL: No, you talked about it, talked about it at me. I wasn't allowed a word in edgeways.

HELEN looks scolded and embarrassed. PHIL looks resigned and continues cleaning. The tension deflates and there is a prolonged silence. Eventually

PHIL gathers up all of the balloons (there is a lot). She takes a cocktail stick out of a cocktail sausage and begins to aggressively pop the balloons.

HELEN: The party poppers are everywhere... (*PHIL continues popping.*) The confetti... (*PHIL continues popping.*) String everywhere... (*The popping intensifies.*) I said, there's string everywhere... (*PHIL continues popping.*) Confetti! (*PHIL continues popping.*) Phil, can you stop that please? (*PHIL continues popping*) PHIL! CAN YOU STOP THAT PLEASE?!

PHIL: (*Pause.*) Stop what?

HELEN: Can you stop popping balloons please?

PHIL: Well, what else do you suggest?

HELEN: What?

PHIL: We can't just leave them here.

HELEN: Leave what here?

PHIL: The balloons.

HELEN: Well, do you have to pop them?

PHIL: No sure, I'll just set them free so, up in the air, up with the fairies. (*Pause. PHIL continues popping.*)

HELEN: NO! PHIL! STOP! PLEASE!

PHIL: What is wrong with you? You're hysterical. You can't bring them home and you can hardly leave them here, I'm not sure the barmen would be too pleased with you.

HELEN: It's just the noise it's... it's very aggressive.

PHIL: Yes, well, that's the noise it makes, so – (*PHIL is about to pop another balloon.*)

HELEN: Later! Please, I'll do it later. I spent ages blowing them up. I... I'll take them home later. (*HELEN gathers up the burst balloons and puts them in the bin. She struggles to put the rest of the inflated balloons in a black sack.*)

PHIL: Strange choice.

HELEN: What?

PHIL: I just think it's strange, that's all.

HELEN: What's strange?

PHIL: That you'd have party poppers and balloons at a party if you don't like loud noises.

HELEN: No I… I suppose I –

PHIL: And, well, I also wonder why you'd have them at your party knowing full well the distress it could potentially cause my son. That didn't come up, was that it? That wasn't a concern, was it not?

HELEN: He picked them out himself.

PHIL: Did he? Well then.

HELEN: Said he always wanted them, was never allowed, that Chris was allowed them but not him.

PHIL: He said that did he? Gary, said that?

HELEN: Yes.

PHIL: Oh please, Helen, you sound like a child.

HELEN: Speaking of… where is, was, Chris?

PHIL: What?

HELEN: Chris, where was he? We told him about it weeks ago, at Sunday dinner. Did you not want him to come? To his own brother's party?

PHIL: Chris is in work.

HELEN: In work? It's a Saturday, Phil, he's a solicitor.

PHIL: He's a trainee; he is worked hard, 12 hour days, weekend work, the lot.

HELEN: Courts open on the weekend? Is that a first? Cause all I've ever seen Chris do on the weekend is cocaine and tequila.

PHIL: You don't know the first thing about Chris... or the legal profession, seemingly.

HELEN: Yeah well, he's high off his tits, every time I've met him so yeah you're right, I probably don't know the first thing about Chris.

PHIL: (*Pause.*) Chris's issues are his own and you are not family, Helen, don't forget it.

HELEN: I –

PHIL: That's enough now, enough.

HELEN: I'm sorry I didn't... I'm sorry (*PHIL gets a sweeping brush. Helen is taking photos off the wall.*) This is a lovely photo, Phil. Where was it taken? (*Silence.*) It's one of Gary's favourites, keeps it on his bedside locker. But you'd know that... wouldn't you, of course you would. I think it's the colours in it he likes. (*Beat.*) Were you on holidays? In the photo?

PHIL: (*Looking at the photo reticently.*) Community Games.

HELEN: I didn't know Gary was in the community games!

PHIL: Gary wasn't in the Community Games...

HELEN: Oh, Chris then, was it?

PHIL: Yes, Chris.

HELEN: Was it football or...

PHIL: Everything. Chris did everything. That was a final I think, GAA.

HELEN: Oh... Cool. Where was it held?

PHIL: Butlin's.

HELEN: Oh, Mosney?

PHIL: No, Butlin's.

HELEN: Oh, sorry it's just… Butlin's became Mosney.

PHIL: Never heard of it.

HELEN: Haven't you? They renamed it in the 90s so I'd… I'd say it was probably Mosney around then. (*Silence.*) Course it's a refugee camp now, direct provision.

PHIL: What?

HELEN: Mosney… Butlin's. Yeah, it's a… it's a refugee camp.

PHIL: A refugee camp?

HELEN: Yeah, they house refugees, well people seeking asy –

PHIL: I know what a refugee camp is, Helen, thank you. (*Beat.*) I didn't know there was one there though.

HELEN: Yeah, for a while now, actually.

PHIL: Hmmm, it's well for them.

HELEN: Well… it's not exactly ideal, is it?

PHIL: Better than some container on a boat.

HELEN: Better if there were no containing at all.

PHIL: Yes, but at the same time you don't know what they've been through, what sort of hell it is they've come from, the stuff they've seen, what post-traumatic stress they're under. Butlin's may not be a sanctuary but it's a damn sight better than whatever minefield they've ran from.

HELEN: But is it required to have them cordoned off like that?

PHIL: Or what? Throw them out in the city centre and watch them fend for themselves? Oh that's what you'd do, Helen, we know that's what you'd do; you'd have no problem with that. (*HELEN groans.*) Is that other one a camp now too?

HELEN: What one?

PHIL: You know the one. It had a dinosaur for its mascot?

HELEN: Barney?

PHIL: No, no but similar and deliberately so I'd imagine, a copycat. It was in Cork, Kerry maybe…

HELEN: Trabolgan? It was a crocodile, I think.

PHIL: Yes, that was it. Trabolgan. That was a good one, much better than Butlin's… Mosney, whatever. I assume that's not a refugee camp now too?

HELEN: If it is, I certainly haven't heard.

PHIL: Yeah, I liked that place. Loads for the kids to do, restaurants were grand and the entertainment in the evening was nice. Only problem with it was having to go to Cork. (*They laugh.*)

HELEN: Poor Cork, it's not so bad. We went there too. There were those mad waves in the swimming pool, and the bowling? It was the Irish Equivalent of Disneyland that place. Just trade the mouse for the crocodile and space mountain for the quad bikes. (*They laugh.*) It's mad though, isn't it? To think me and Gary might have been there at the same time and would never have known.

PHIL: (*Beat.*) Yes… well those were the only type of holidays we could go on. There were provisions there that places like Majorca and Ibiza couldn't provide. Travelling with Gary was never an option.

HELEN: I went to Paris last year, Phil. Me and Gary went to Paris last year and we didn't drive there, we didn't swim there, didn't cycle. We flew there. But of course you know that considering you followed us to the airport and insisted on breaking any regulations with airport security as you could. And why did you do that, Phil? So you could see us to our gate? Wish us well on our travels? Or inflict as much anxiety as possible to our journey.

PHIL: And was it a success, your holiday?

HELEN: Was it a failure?

PHIL: You drugged him.

HELEN: I did not drug him, Phil. The doctor gave him the diazepam / in case he needed it, to ensure the journey went okay, he gave him the diazepam, prescribed it, so he took it.

PHIL: (*Mockingly.*) The doctor gave him the diazepam. Oh, please, Helen. I tried to explain to you why it wasn't wise to throw him that far out of his comfort zone. Drugging is not coping, it's ignorance, pure ignorance on your part and whatever doctor you decided to go to.

HELEN: It was your GP, Phil, Gary's GP, where do you think I'd take him? The North Dublin cartel?

PHIL: I'd expect you to ask me first.

HELEN: I didn't need to ask you, Gary did it himself.

PHIL: Gary did it himself, well Gary never did it himself before you showed up, so what else do you expect me to think?

HELEN: And why was that, Phil? Cause you didn't let him, you didn't let him do anything for himself.

PHIL: Like what? I didn't leave him in town past midnight, alone, to fend for himself? How dare I!

HELEN: It was an accident.

PHIL: It's always an accident.

HELEN: Oh always, it's always an accident. I'm nothing but one big accident, Phil.

PHIL: (*Mumbling.*) Never again.

HELEN: Never again, never again, okay, well, you can add that to your list so. Your never agains.

PHIL: I've been so hard on you? Have I? (*Beat.*) Do you think any other mother in their right mind would have let you near their son after Paris? After leaving him in town on his own three weeks ago and now tonight? Most of my problem, Helen, is that you haven't listened to a word I've said, you don't listen to a word I say. You know best and that's all that matters. Never mind I've spent 25 years raising him, dealing with him, it, every day. So I'm sorry Helen but if I say never again this time, it's nothing but overdue and your failing to see that is your own doing. Do you have any idea what it's been like?

HELEN: (*Interrupting.*) No, no, you're dead right. I've no idea. I've been in this relationship, what, two years now and I've no idea, Phil. I finally see that now, so thanks. Thanks for that. (*Beat.*) Look, you should head off. I'll deal with this, the cleaning and everything, you can just... leave.

PHIL looks at her and picks up the sweeping brush and sweeps.

PHIL: I don't want things like this, Helen. You may think I do but I don't.

HELEN: Well, what exactly do you want, Phil?

PHIL: (*Beat.*) I...

HELEN: Look, this is... it's my mess, I'll clear it. You don't need to... I'm sure you're tired.

PHIL: You can't handle this, not on your own.

HELEN: What exactly is it that I can't handle? Spilt crisps and burst balloons. It's my mess, my party, my mistake, I'll be fine. Just head off.

PHIL: (*Beat.*) I'm not leaving my son's birthday party in this state. Anyway, Bill is coming back for me once Gary's been settled. (*Beat.*) Cleaners weren't included in the price, no?

HELEN: The room was free as long as I cleaned it myself. (*Beat.*) It seemed like a good deal at the time.

PHIL: Free if you're willing to pay 7 euro for a glass of wine. (*Beat.*) It was nice though... I only had a glass but it was nice.

HELEN: I'll make sure the staff are informed.

PHIL: Dublin prices, I suppose... like you said. (*Beat.*) I grew up in a pub. Did you know that?

HELEN: No.

PHIL: Oh yeah, I've seen it all. All sorts, drunks, thieves, gamblers, poachers and that was just my father. (*HELEN laughs quietly and politely.*) It's a strange life, pulling pints before you can ride a bike. I don't like pubs though. I don't like them and maybe I bring a certain amount of personal prejudice with that, when it comes to my sons.

HELEN: That's life though, isn't it? Pubs are just part of the infrastructure. In Ireland anyway…

PHIL: Still I can think of better uses of time.

HELEN: Gary doesn't drink, Phil.

PHIL: That's not what I was –

HELEN: He doesn't, I wouldn't let him drink…

PHIL: You wouldn't let him?

HELEN: I mean he doesn't want to, he doesn't like drink, he doesn't want to drink, Phil.

PHIL: Great and you made up his mind for him on this, did you? It must only be me you have a problem with doing that for him.

HELEN: What I meant was if I saw him trying it I'd ask him why he thought he wanted to, I would help him make the right decision.

PHIL: That doesn't sound like you, Helen. Surely Gary is well able to fend for himself, make those decisions for himself. Isn't that it? Amn't I the scary monster that's been stopping him all these years from living a life of his own?

HELEN: I don't think that, Phil. You know I don't think that.

PHIL: Well, you seem to. You seem to think it's fine leaving him stranded in the middle of town at twelve at night, I'm the one that's been stopping him living life to the fullest, not dropping him in the middle of Grafton Street after dark.

HELEN: I apologised, Phil. That was weeks ago and I apologised. How many more times do I have to –

PHIL: Apologies aren't enough, Helen! After... I expected something, some gesture that you knew you'd done something wrong, that you should have listened to me but no... nothing! And then tonight? What kind of fool am I? What do you take me for?

HELEN: I told you it was my fault. I got annoyed, frustrated and I didn't mean to, but it happened.

PHIL: It's not good enough.

HELEN: We're going round in circles, I don't know what else I can do, Phil, please! (*Beat.*) He just, he wouldn't stop stroking her arm, he wouldn't stop it, I know why... I understand why the stroking I know that, Phil. But I cracked and I'm sorry.

PHIL: Gary can't help his impulses Helen, you know that!

HELEN: I know, I know, I do, Christ I didn't get into this without reading a few books okay? It's sensory, I know that, he feels, he likes the feel, I know and that's why I'm so... ashamed, embarrassed and I don't know... but it was her, he was doing it to her, he could have stroked anyone's arm but it was hers and it's my problem, my issue, I got angry at him, shouted at him and I shouldn't have, it was not his fault it was mine but I made a mistake and I'm so sorry!

PHIL: I'm supposed to believe it would've been okay had it been someone else?

HELEN: She's a bitch, Phil. She made my life miserable, all through school and here I show up ten years later with an autistic boyfriend who insists on stroking her hands? And she just sits there nodding, mumbling, telling me it's fine, smiling smugly cause she knows now she'll be able to add it to her list of reasons why Helen is a fucking weirdo!

Silence.

HELEN: She thinks that, not me, I don't think that.

PHIL: You said it.

HELEN: I said it because that's what someone like her thinks.

PHIL: That's what you think.

HELEN: I don't think that, I just know how it looks.

PHIL: How does it look? Does it look like my son being abandoned in town? Like him being physically removed from McDonald's by a security guard because he's been standing there for two hours and he's beginning to make people feel uncomfortable? That it's frozen him with fear, this man in uniform shouting at him? Is that how it looks? He was thrown out on the street, Helen. My son, thrown and left on the street until someone with half a brain realised he wasn't an arsehole, just a selective mute who's been abandoned in town on his own in the middle of the night and that maybe all he needed was a bit of help getting home.

HELEN: I walked away for ten minutes, Phil. I walked away, I came back and he was gone.

PHIL: It doesn't matter how long you walked away for, Helen, it was long enough to have him returned to my house in a Garda car and that's the end of it. All the neighbours gawking out their windows, looking at him, at me, at what kind of mother I am to let my son, my vulnerable son out so late that he's brought home by the guards, like I couldn't give a shit about him, like I haven't dedicated every day of my life since he was born to making sure he's safe, you've made me look that way, made me seem negligent and unloving, because every time you come to pick him up from my house, I give you that power, that privilege, do you have any idea what it feels like? To have it thrown back in my face, when it's the hardest, hardest thing I've… to give him to you.

HELEN: You haven't given him to me; you can't give him to anyone.

PHIL: I have put him in your care.

HELEN: He's not yours to put! (*Beat.*) I love him. (*PHIL mutters and shakes her head.*) What is it about that that you don't get? (*Beat.*) I think love is quite simple really.

PHIL: Love is, autism isn't.

HELEN: (*Beat.*) Look, the party got too much for Gary tonight. It got too much for him and I'm sorry about that.

PHIL: Of course it got too much for him, Helen. Of course it did.

HELEN: I know, I said that it did, I just said that.

PHIL: Helen, I told you, I told you it would, and you didn't listen. You saw what we do for his birthdays, you saw last year. A cake in the kitchen and he's happy, he's able for it, this is not fair, Helen, it's not fair on him and it's not fair for you not to listen to what's best for him.

HELEN: He was tired. Tonight he was tired, there were lots of people here and he got overwhelmed and he was tired.

PHIL: That's not what tired looks like, Helen. You know it's not what tired looks like. He could have hurt someone tonight and more importantly he could have hurt himself. If you'd've followed suit and given him a birthday he can enjoy then none of this would've happened. But that wasn't good enough for you, wasn't it not? And, truly, I'm not disputing the friends being here if that's what they are but if you could've organised a gathering, one that he can handle, one where they don't have to see him at his worst.

HELEN: It's not his worst, it's who he is, and I, we, all understand that and I don't know why you can't!

PHIL: Are you this delusional, Helen? I mean what is this about? I've been wracking my brain about it since you arrived since this started but I just can't seem to put my finger on it.

Does he make you feel better about yourself, or something? There could be worse things than that borne out of a relationship, but as a reason to start one, I… can't understand. Does he make you feel special? Good about yourself? A boyfriend should, I suppose as long as it's the right reasons why, but I've seen this before. Not this, I've never allowed this before, but with some of his carers, his teachers, friends. They feel like they're some sort of whisperer, a shaman, a druid, a gift they've been given, which is fine for me when they're showering him with attention, fine for them as long as he's making them feel good about themselves but then… well.

HELEN: I'm not other people, Phil.

PHIL: No but you are a person, you're not a god, Helen, you have no superpowers, neither do I. He will wear thin.

HELEN: I love him.

PHIL: We have choices as modern women. No need to feel blessed some yob has talked to you in a dance hall; we have choices, Helen, you and I. We can make the right decisions for ourselves, find someone to take care of us, to love us because indifference is worse than anger, it's the worst, it's heart breaking.

HELEN: What are you saying?

PHIL: I'm saying I don't get it and I can't trust it.

HELEN: Do you not love him?

PHIL: He's my son.

HELEN: I said do you not love him?

PHIL: Of course I do.

HELEN: Then why is it so difficult for you to believe that I do too?

PHIL: That's not what I meant.

HELEN: It is though, what you meant. It's that you are the only one capable of loving him because you're his mother. That's what you think of him, of us.

PHIL: You're putting words in my mouth now, Helen.

HELEN: I'm not, not really. I just think it's funny that you think I'd put up with all this shit for a few gratifying words every now and then and I'm not referring to Gary, Phil, I'm referring to you. You don't get it and that's fine but I don't get you, either. Has Gary been happier since I've known him?

PHIL: Look at this place!

HELEN: No, this is not about tonight. Has Gary been happier since I've known him, Phil? (*Beat.*) Cause I've been happier... since I've known him. And I like to think I've seen a change in him, too. I have... I've been... I... Have I ever told you how me and Gary met? (*Beat.*) Have I ever told you how we met? I must've, at the time and all. It was in Costa, on Dame Street, do you remember Gary's placement? I'd go there on my lunch. I can't bear canteens, empty conversations that no one really... I like to get out. (*PHIL is mopping or sweeping.*) Phil, can you stop please?

PHIL: Fine.

HELEN: Thank you. I spend quite a lot of time alone. I still do. I have friends, Gary... I just like head space or something, so I like to do a lot alone, it might be a control thing and maybe it has affected... I'm sorry about tonight.

PHIL: Apologies are –

HELEN: I know, they're not enough and I will try, I promise, but please, listen... I was in Costa, I'd had an awful week, I...

PHIL: Yes?

HELEN: I've never been very good with boyfriends, I suppose some would say I have issues, I just, I don't like touch, I don't like to be touched... (*HELEN waits for a response.*) Which has been hard, for obvious reasons. Which, I'm sure you can imagine... (*HELEN waits for a response.*) But then I met Matt. He was, is, a friend of Sophie's. She was here tonight, black curly hair, did you meet her? No... I... anyway. He was lovely, polite and nice, but then in a weird way and I suppose I've always thought this, or I did, but that... that maybe love is just a matter of proximity, convenience, timing? And I gathered that maybe that was Matt for me and maybe that was okay because maybe I was that for him too. But I don't get any better with the, the touching, I'm not the worst, I don't mind holding his hand and he doesn't mind holding back and it's not that I don't trust him or anything it's just who I am, I suppose, what I've become and he doesn't mind... for a while. He's told me he understands so that's what I believe because he's told me, but then he's drinking. He drank before, just not like this, and all of a sudden I'm a 'bitch' apparently, he apologises for it the next day, he always does until... 'Bitch' becomes my wrist and my wrist becomes my knee and my knee becomes my thigh and he keeps sliding it on up there, there you know and I don't want it. I don't want it there, like that, I haven't asked him for it, and he hasn't asked, and we go through this every time and then, one day, he won't stop, I'm not sure he can and have you ever felt repulsed by somebody who wants you so badly? It's the worst feeling, the worst, filled with bile and fear, nobody wins in that, nobody, I mean you want to but you don't and that's, it's not... and he's crying in frustration, bitter tears he's trying to hold back like they're knives slicing his mouth, and he's upset I see that but I... and in a blind rage he flings me and I can't... I'm just there and he's... (*Beat.*) And it's not his fault. In some weird way, I've brought him to this. He hates himself now because I've made him into something he's not, something he hates and these are my problems my issues and I shouldn't be... it isn't fair to bring somebody into this, what happened I...(*PHIL is now listening intently.*) And a week or so later I'm in the Costa on Dame Street, where Gary is and I'm feeling completely lost like I don't know what I could, would do and all of a sudden I feel this stretch of warmth coming over me and I look down and it's Gary's hand, his hand on mine and I've never felt so at peace with myself or... and we just stay like that for ages, me and him, no need for words or anything and I think we both knew that day that this was something special, something we wanted to hold on to and we did. We do, both of us every day, because it's love. (*Pause.*)

PHIL: Helen... I don't know I... Are you having sex with my son?

HELEN: What?

PHIL: I understand that that was difficult for you but... are you... having sex with my son?

HELEN: How can you ask me that?

PHIL: How can I not?

HELEN: What?

PHIL: Look, Helen, what happened, that sounds awful. Truly it does, but I need you to answer my question.

HELEN: Did you not hear a word I just said?

PHIL: I heard and I'm concerned, but now I am both concerned for Gary and you. It's quite important that I know Helen and I'd like you to tell me.

HELEN: Would you ask Chris's girlfriend these kinds of questions?

PHIL: That's different Helen; you have to see how that's different. You've clearly been through something terrible; I'm not doubting that but these things they're damaging particularly if you don't deal with them.

HELEN: I didn't do anything.

PHIL: I'm not saying you did, but you've gone through something and I need to know how you've dealt with that, I need to know what you're doing with my son, Helen.

HELEN: Would it be the worst thing if we were?

PHIL: So you are.

HELEN: I didn't say that.

PHIL: Well, what are you saying?

HELEN: I'm saying we're in a loving relationship and that we love each other because we do.

PHIL: So yes.

HELEN: I'm not saying that.

PHIL: I think you just have.

HELEN: No, what I'm saying is, would it be the worst thing if we were?

PHIL: Please tell me you're not.

HELEN: I'm not telling you anything, it's none of your business and from the way you've spoken to me tonight you're lucky I'm even talking to you.

PHIL: I don't think you understand what you're saying if you are saying what I think you are... *(Beat.)* This makes things different, you have to see that it is different...

HELEN: And if I hadn't told you? Would it have been different then?

PHIL: It wasn't even an option before then, not a question.

HELEN: Of course it's a question, Phil, he's my boyfriend.

PHIL: Stop saying that like it's normal.

HELEN: It is! It is to me and it should be to you, too.

PHIL: Do you not think I want that? That I don't want my son to be normal?

HELEN: What is normal? Because you aren't, this isn't. You throw words around like vulnerable and normal as if it's an excuse, a speed bump but we're all vulnerable, Phil. No one is safe, just doing their best and I don't mind you not liking me if I thought for a second you'd taken time to get to know me, but you haven't. Your only interest in me has been my interest in Gary. Like I'm not important, like I'm not independent of my relationships, that that's how I'm to be defined and little else and it isn't fair, Phil. You say I don't listen, but do you listen to me? Have you heard me tell you that I love your son because I do, I love him.

PHIL: *(Quietly.)* He doesn't know what love is.

HELEN: What –

PHIL: That's not, I didn't...

HELEN: Of course, he does Phil, he loves you... *(Awkward silence. Phil half-heartedly resumes cleaning.)* I want this to work, really, I do. I don't want whatever this tete-a-tete thing that it's become. I'd like us to be... to work together, I want it to work, Phil.

PHIL: *(Beat.)* I get that, but it won't, and that's... that's not your fault, Helen. Really, it's not and I don't mean it to be cruel because it's not that, I wouldn't want it to. *(Beat.)* You must think me heartless and I don't blame you. I have hardened over the years, I know that, and I'm sorry and I admit I find it difficult to let go of my son, sons, a normal enough emotion for most mothers, I'd imagine. I have commended your efforts, your positivity and I mean that when I say it because I have, you can ask Bill. It's why I've tried, allowed it to go on as long as I have, I've admired it, envied it even. And I believe, you believe when you say what happened here tonight won't happen again, that leaving him in town won't happen again, that the diazepam won't happen again. I believe you think that, I believe you do, but it will. It will happen again, all of them will happen again and it won't be your fault, it's no one's fault but it will. It's a reaction and despite Gary's lack of intent when these... things... happen, it doesn't mean that they don't hurt because they do, we're human and yes we may not be as vulnerable as Gary but we're not perfect either, you're going to slip up, it will happen. When Gary was young, I had certain expectations, certain hopes and dreams for my son, but gradually as the years go on, Helen, they've all... They all just erode away. Not that I don't have hopes or dreams for him anymore, it's just the expectations change, the achievements change and that hasn't been easy for me to accept, to face up to, but I have and I've had to because, unlike you, I've no choice. (*Beat.*) But it is a choice I happily make because I love my son, I understand him, his needs, I get them because I've had to, to make our home life work and you can say what you want about my... about Chris, but our home hasn't been easy and he's done his best. I've been waiting for that Garda car outside my house since the day you and Gary first met. I think that's why I'm so angry about all this and really I'm not angry at you, not really, I'm more angry at myself, truth be told, because I knew this would happen because how could it not? I understand on the whole, on everything, that it's not your fault and I'm sorry for some of my actions tonight, but autism is frustrating, it is frustrating for those diagnosed with it and it is frustrating for those who love them. I've been stood in your position many times, standing in shopping centres, watching on as my six-year-old son is screaming his head off, shouting at anyone that passes cause he doesn't know what else to do, that it's all too much... and he's throwing plastic Noddys filled with bubble bath at everything around him, throwing anything he can find, but I'm trying and everyone's gawking at him, at me, at what's going to happen next and they're shouting at us, me and my six-year-old to stop, asking me to control him but how can I? I still can't. And all I can think about is leaving, leaving him there alone. Let someone else deal with the problem. Do you know what that feels like as a mother? To want to abandon your own son? And people are shouting at me and all I want is for my child to get back in the buggy but I've upset him, obviously, I've upset him, why else, why would he, what did I do? And he's in agony, shouting and crying and banging his fists against his head, putting himself in danger, hitting his poor head, his beautiful little face and what have I done? What have I done? And why can't I make it better and why can't I just leave… but I don't leave, I don't leave cause he's my son and I love him. And that might have been twenty odd years ago and I might not be able to say that our lives have gotten any easier but the difference is, I didn't leave, I don't leave, I'll never leave. (*Beat.*) I won't stand in your way, I'll try not to, I'll let whatever it is that this is go on till it's over if I can't stop it here and now, but, Helen, and I mean this, don't think for a second that I'm not watching every move you make with my son.

HELEN: Okay.

PHIL and HELEN resume cleaning in silence. They finish. PHIL takes her coat and looks at HELEN. PHIL leaves. HELEN is alone, she stands still, looking pensive. She eventually picks up the bags of decorations and food, turns off the lights, and leaves.

THE END

Wringer

Stewart Roche

A Bewley's Café Theatre commission first produced in October 2018.

DIRECTOR: Aoife Spillane-Hinks
DESIGNER: Naomi Faughnan
LIGHTING DESIGNER: Colm Maher
MUSIC/SOUND: Mark Hendricks
STAGE MANAGER: Gill Buckle

CHARACTERS & CAST:

ELSA: Maeve Fitzgerald

MRS NEWMAN: Joan Sheehy

JONATHAN RAVENCLIFFE: Michael James Ford

Stewart Roche's first play, *Curious Tales for Christmas,* had its world premiere at Theatre Upstairs in December 2012 and was published by Black Box Theatre Publishing. His adaptation of Bram Stoker's short story 'The Judge's House' ran in Bewley's Café Theatre in 2013. A subsequent production came runner-up in the All-Ireland One Act Finals. His first original full-length play, *Revenant,* had its world premiere in the New Theatre in November 2013 and was nominated for the Stewart Parker Award. Other plays include *Variance, Tracer* and *Snake Eaters.* In August 2018, his play, *The Fetch Wilson,* premiered at the Pleasance as part of the Edinburgh Fringe Festival.

SCENE 1

ELSA enters the stage. She's in her twenties, partial to dark clothing and sports a horror-themed T-shirt. She speaks on a phone.

ELSA: Yeah, I'm here now. (*Beat.*) An hour ago. (*Beat.*) I know, I know. The goddamn satnav is useless – (*Beat.*) Yeah on the – (*Beat.*) Well no because – (*Beat.*) Between Knocknagore and Bansha. That's what she said. Bansha. Yes it's a real place. (*Beat.*) I don't know. I can't imagine he has anything else lined up for this evening. (*Beat.*) Of course I'm sure. I've waited long enough to do this – (*Beat.*) In the email. Yes – (*Beat.*) I understand. Okay. Got to go. Make sure you keep your phone on. (*She hangs up the phone. Looks at the house.*) Jesus.

She takes in the house for a bit, sneaks in a selfie and eventually presses the doorbell. After quite some time it is answered by MRS NEWMAN. She could be anything from 45-65.

NEWMAN: Yes?

ELSA: Hi. Elsa –

NEWMAN: Elsa?

ELSA: Yes. Elsa Crenshaw.

NEWMAN: Oh. Yes. The ehm…

ELSA: Blogger.

NEWMAN: Ah. Yes. The blogger. (*She checks her watch.*) You're late.

ELSA: Yeah. Sorry. Got lost back at the petrol station. I think I took the second right at the roundabout rather –

NEWMAN: You should have called.

ELSA: What?

NEWMAN: You should have called. The house.

ELSA: Yeah, I should have. Stubborn. Thought I'd be able to work it out myself. The directions. Between the satnav and my –

NEWMAN: More usually a male trait.

ELSA: Stubbornness?

NEWMAN: Stubbornness over directions. It's more usually associated with the male.

ELSA: Right.

NEWMAN: (*Beat.*) You're not the first. Visitor to get lost at that roundabout.

ELSA: Do you get many visitors –

NEWMAN: More than I'd like.

ELSA: (*Beat.*) So is he here? Mr Ravencliffe?

NEWMAN: He's in his study. Dealing with some… correspondence.

ELSA: Fan mail?

NEWMAN: What?

ELSA: Is he answering fan mail?

NEWMAN: Yes. Yes, I believe he is. If you'd like to follow me. (*MRS NEWMAN gestures for ELSA to follow her. They enter the house.*)

ELSA: (*Offstage*) Oh – is that his real name? I thought I'd be able to dig it up somewhere but –

NEWMAN: (*Offstage*) That's the name he answers to.

ELSA: (*Offstage*) Right. But seriously – (*They enter the study. RAVENCLIFFE is seated by the fire, signing publicity stills. The walls are adorned by old movie posters. Most of them are slightly garish horrors.*)

NEWMAN: Miss Elsa Crenshaw.

RAVENCLIFFE looks up from his seat, stands, approaches ELSA and shakes her hand. He is also difficult to put an exact age on and his accent is hard to place.

ELSA: Mister Ravencliffe.

RAVENCLIFFE: Miss Crenshaw. Please sit down. (*ELSA does so.*) Can I get you anything? A drink? Wine, coffee, a mineral water, perhaps?

ELSA: Would you have a Coke? Diet preferably.

RAVENCLIFFE: I'm not, I eh…

NEWMAN: No. We don't have Coke, diet or otherwise.

ELSA: Not to worry.

RAVENCLIFFE: Cordial?

ELSA: (*Beat.*) What eh, what is that, exactly?

RAVENCLIFFE: (*To MRS NEWMAN*) It's ehm, it's… how would you describe a cordial, Mrs Newman?

NEWMAN: A cordial is like squash. Fruit squash.

ELSA: Okay.

NEWMAN: I believe we have elderflower.

ELSA: (*Beat.*) I think I'll just go with coffee.

RAVENCLIFFE: A coffee and a glass of wine please. (*MRS NEWMAN nods and exits.*) So. Here you are.

ELSA: Yes.

RAVENCLIFFE: Did you have some difficulty with Mrs Newman's directions?

ELSA: That was on me really. (*RAVENCLIFFE smiles.*) She said I wasn't the first. To get lost at the roundabout.

RAVENCLIFFE: No. You wouldn't be.

ELSA: Do you have frequent visitors?

RAVENCLIFFE: Frequent would be pushing it. I do try to see as many of my ehm –

ELSA: Fans?

RAVENCLIFFE: I suppose you would call them that. I try to see as many as I can, as I said. If they've made the effort to come all this way, then it's the least I can do. We are off the beaten track, as you've discovered yourself eh?

ELSA: Yeah. I was surprised that people were able to locate you. To track you down.

RAVENCLIFFE: You managed it.

ELSA: After some difficulty.

RAVENCLIFFE: (*He gestures to the posters on the walls.*) Fans of the horror genre are nothing if not resourceful, Miss Crenshaw.

ELSA: I have to say, your house looks exactly how I imagined it.

RAVENCLIFFE: (*Smiling.*) Thank you. I think.

ELSA: Oh it's a compliment. Hopefully we can take a few pictures to give my readers a visual reference but it really is something. Tell me – is it haunted?

RAVENCLIFFE: It certainly has its moments.

ELSA: I'm curious as to the posters on the wall that aren't your own movies. *The Old Dark House*.

RAVENCLIFFE: A masterpiece. James Whale's finest hour.

ELSA: Right. But the other one, at least I think it's the only other one that isn't yours –

RAVENCLIFFE: It is the only other one that isn't mine –

ELSA: Is *Hellraiser*.

RAVENCLIFFE: Yes.

ELSA: In Italian.

RAVENCLIFFE: Indeed.

ELSA: Why that one?

RAVENCLIFFE: It belonged to my ex-wife. Well, she thought it did.

ELSA: I see.

RAVENCLIFFE: It had actually been given to me. If you look closely you'll see it's been signed by Clive Barker. (*ELSA leans in closer to look at the poster.*)

ELSA: Wow.

RAVENCLIFFE: During the messy divorce proceedings – made messy in the main by her – this picture took on similar importance to that of the Rhineland after the First World War. In the end it took a letter from Barker stating that it was indeed mine for me to hold on to it. So now it takes pride of place in my living room, there for all to see.

ELSA: But not your ex-wife.

RAVENCLIFFE: A visit from her would indeed be a surprise. She died three years ago.

ELSA: Oh. (*Beat.*) We might get back to the divorce later.

RAVENCLIFFE: I'd prefer if we didn't.

MRS NEWMAN enters the room with the drinks.

NEWMAN: Will that be all, Mr Ravencliffe?

RAVENCLIFFE: Yes, Mrs Newman, thank you.

MRS NEWMAN exits. ELSA takes a sip of her coffee.

ELSA: I wonder if I might ask a favour?

RAVENCLIFFE: Of course.

ELSA: It's a bit, I don't know, silly.

RAVENCLIFFE: I doubt that.

ELSA: You see those headshots? Would you sign one for me?

RAVENCLIFFE: Absolutely. That isn't silly at all. (*He goes and gets one and is about to sign it but stops.*)

ELSA: What?

RAVENCLIFFE: If it's alright with you I'm going to wait for a while before I inscribe it. Until I get to know you a bit better. That way it'll be personal, unique. (*ELSA shrugs.*) Now – do you wish to start? It's just I have a previous engagement for this evening and what with you being delayed –

ELSA: Oh. Eh, yes, one second. (*She takes out her phone, fiddles about with it.*)

RAVENCLIFFE: Is that all you need?

ELSA: Pretty much. The quality is fine on this. Okay, as I'm going to write up the intro I don't need to give you one here so we can jump straight into it.

RAVENCLIFFE: Alright.

ELSA: (*Pause. She then indicates that she has started taping.*) Okay, so let's start at the beginning. Childhood, was it –

RAVENCLIFFE: Lately, when I purchase a biography, I've found myself skipping on to the person's university years. At the very earliest.

ELSA: Really?

RAVENCLIFFE: Really. Can't for the life of me understand why anyone would find another person's childhood remotely interesting.

ELSA: Formative years, I suppose, lots of clues as to the type of person –

RAVENCLIFFE: I'm not sure the number of times I fought with my sister or what I did to her Sindy dolls will tell you anything about the type of person I became.

ELSA: Alright. (*She thinks for a moment.*) When did you know you wanted to become an actor? If it happened during your childhood, then we –

RAVENCLIFFE: University. I was studying English, but hadn't a clue as to what I really wanted to do with my life. A friend suggested I go along with him to the dramatic society for an audition. I hadn't much interest, but I was told it was a good place to meet girls. And boys.

ELSA: Was it?

RAVENCLIFFE: Oh yes. Yes. (*Smiling to himself.*) It was wonderful. I started off with small parts, gradually worked my way up. By the time I was in my final year, I was playing Jimmy Porter in *Look Back in Anger*. Do you know it?

ELSA: Not really. Theatre isn't really my thing.

RAVENCLIFFE: Oh. Right. Well, this was in the time when a production in one of the leading colleges would still attract serious attention. We even got reviewed by a national newspaper. Who loved the production. And particularly loved me.

ELSA: Wow.

RAVENCLIFFE: It was my big break really.

ELSA: Was that directed by Peter De Courcy?

RAVENCLIFFE: Yes. More on him later, I imagine.

ELSA: If you're okay –

RAVENCLIFFE: You can't really tell my story without telling Peter's. (*Beat.*) So, classic play, huge hit, great reviews, casting directors and agents getting the train down to see it. I had my pick of them. Unfortunately, I picked Millie. Raving alcoholic. Even by agents' standards, she was an absolute – (*There is a sharp knock on the door.*) Sorry about this. (*ELSA pauses the recording.*) Come in, Mrs Newman, please. At least I hope it's Mrs – (*MRS NEWMAN enters.*)

NEWMAN: It's 5.30.

RAVENCLIFFE: Is it? And?

NEWMAN: You wanted me to remind you about the eh…

RAVENCLIFFE: Oh right. (*He realises what MRS NEWMAN is talking about and gets up.*) If you'll excuse me for a moment, Miss Crenshaw?

ELSA: Of course.

MRS NEWMAN and RAVENCLIFFE leave. ELSA sits for a moment, pauses the recording and then gets up and has a look around the room, inspecting various items. As a horror fan the paraphernalia in the room is very impressive to her. She checks a drawer, it's locked. She goes around to where RAVENCLIFFE had been sitting, thinks about trying out his chair and then does so. Finally RAVENCLIFFE returns carrying a plate with peculiar looking food on it. She springs back up.

RAVENCLIFFE: Hungry?

ELSA: Famished.

RAVENCLIFFE: Excellent. Mrs Newman has prepared us some hors d'oeuvres. And you must have a small glass of wine.

ELSA: I couldn't.

RAVENCLIFFE: Oh?

ELSA: Driving, I'm afraid.

RAVENCLIFFE: Of course.

ELSA: (*She checks her watch.*) Actually, we really should get started again. It's getting late. (*She starts recording again.*)

RAVENCLIFFE: Look, I'm just going to put this out there –

ELSA: Mmm?

RAVENCLIFFE: We've barely scratched the surface and there seems little point in dragging you all the way back down here again so…

ELSA: So?

RAVENCLIFFE: You're more than welcome to stay here this evening.

ELSA: Ehm, that's a very kind offer –

RAVENCLIFFE: It makes sense.

ELSA: Well –

RAVENCLIFFE: Unless of course you have plans for the morning? In which case I totally understand.

ELSA: I, eh, I don't have plans, no.

RAVENCLIFFE: That's settled then.

ELSA: (*Who doesn't seem particularly comfortable, in truth.*) Yeah, yeah, sure. Just have to eh, text my boyfriend, tell him about the change of plan. (*RAVENCLIFFE smiles. ELSA picks up her phone and sends a text.*) What happened to your previous engagement?

RAVENCLIFFE: What? Oh, cancelled. Mrs Newman, if you could make up the guest room?

NEWMAN: Of course, sir.

RAVENCLIFFE: And perhaps another bottle of wine. The Clos de Vougeot this time, I think.

NEWMAN: The '05 or the '06?

RAVENCLIFFE: The '05.

NEWMAN: Sir. (*MRS NEWMAN leaves.*)

ELSA: You might be drinking that bottle on your own.

RAVENCLIFFE: Why's that?

ELSA: I'm not much of a drinker normally.

RAVENCLIFFE: Really?

ELSA: Comes with the territory.

RAVENCLIFFE: Oh?

ELSA: Child of an alcoholic. Recovering alcoholic to give her her dues.

RAVENCLIFFE: Ah.

ELSA: The second bottle usually meant I was going to have to make my own lunch for school.

RAVENCLIFFE: I shall send it back to the cellar.

ELSA: It's fine, honestly.

RAVENCLIFFE: You're sure?

ELSA: Absolutely.

MRS NEWMAN comes back with a dusty bottle of wine. She pours a glass for RAVENCLIFFE and makes to pour one for ELSA. RAVENCLIFFE goes to stop her.

RAVENCLIFFE: Elsa doesn't –

ELSA: A small one won't kill me.

RAVENCLIFFE: That's the spirit.

MRS NEWMAN pours her a small glass, tidies up and then leaves.

ELSA: (*She starts recording again.*) What's the significance of the eh, whatsit, over the mantelpiece? (*ELSA takes a sip of her wine.*)

RAVENCLIFFE: That? That is a whip from my very first horror movie, *Demons of the Mind*.

ELSA: Hammer, right?

RAVENCLIFFE: Right.

ELSA: A whip, Hammer, sounds pretty –

RAVENCLIFFE: No such luck. I was just a coachman. I drove a carriage up to Baron Zorn. Played by Robert Hardy. You know, *All Creatures Great and Small, Winston Churchill*, and ehm…

ELSA: He was Cornelius Fudge.

RAVENCLIFFE: He was what now?

ELSA: Cornelius Fudge. In *Harry Potter*.

RAVENCLIFFE: Oh. I never saw it.

ELSA: Saw them you mean. There were nine in total. I think. The last book was split in two so I'm not sure, it might have been… Anyway, you'd have probably recognised half the cast. (*Responding to RAVENCLIFFE's puzzled look.*) A lot of them were your contemporaries. The Potter series sort of became an unofficial pension fund for British character actors of a certain…

RAVENCLIFFE: Vintage?

ELSA: Yes. (*Beat.*) That was late Hammer?

RAVENCLIFFE: Indeed. *Demons of the Mind* was the second last horror film they released.

ELSA: The last was *To the Devil a Daughter* in 1976.

RAVENCLIFFE: Very good.

ELSA: Your first speaking role.

RAVENCLIFFE: Yes. I was delighted to have graduated to a named character –

ELSA: Three lines.

RAVENCLIFFE: Indeed. But it wasn't long before I realised we were deeply in the shit. The film was a desperate attempt to cling on to the coat-tails of *The Exorcist* and *The Omen*. Christopher Lee was reaching the end of his tether and Richard Widmark spent more time storming off set than actually on it.

ELSA: Quite an introduction to the film business.

RAVENCLIFFE: I loved it though. Once you saw past the ridiculousness of the plots and the carry-on, it was tremendous fun. And Lee was a consummate professional, taught me an awful lot. (*Bea*t.) Sadly it made about 20 quid in the box office and Hammer wasn't long for this world.

ELSA: (*Sipping her wine.*) Was it that big a flop?

RAVENCLIFFE: The writing had been on the wall for some time. Try as they might the old Hammer magic was no more. They were just churning out rubbish, of which I was in two beauties. I was terribly sad when it folded though, it had become something of a family.

ELSA: So then you…

RAVENCLIFFE: Did a few cigar adverts and went back to the theatre, for a time. Rep, mainly in Manchester. Would have been happy enough to stay there too if it hadn't been for –

ELSA: Peter De Courcy?

RAVENCLIFFE: (*Changing the subject.*) I've read some of the articles on your ehm…

ELSA: Blog.

RAVENCLIFFE: Yes, your blog. I was impressed, I have to say.

ELSA: Cheers.

RAVENCLIFFE: I particularly enjoyed the one about *Rawhead Rex*.

ELSA: The very definition of a cult classic.

RAVENCLIFFE: I'm not sure I'd go that far, but still, it was very well written. The blog now, not *Rawhead Rex*. And written with real conviction. A quality I've always admired.

ELSA: Thank you. That means a lot coming from you. Someone of your standing, I mean. (*Slightly awkward moment.*) I have one I'm publishing this Friday you might be interested in.

RAVENCLIFFE: Oh?

ELSA: It's about the absence of Folk Horror from the Irish canon and its impact on the – (*She points towards something on his desk.*) I'm sorry, I have to ask – is that what I think it is?

RAVENCLIFFE: If you're thinking *Fangoria* magazine's lifetime achievement award then yes, yes it is.

ELSA: Oh my God…

RAVENCLIFFE: Pick it up. It's alright. (*He gestures to her to pick it up. She does so with great care.*) Don't worry, he's sturdy enough. And worth all the fuss. (*ELSA examines the statue with relish.*) I was – in the magazine's own words –

ELSA: The most controversial choice in the award's history.

RAVENCLIFFE: Probably because I was still alive when they gave it to me.

ELSA: Well, I think you deserved it.

RAVENCLIFFE: Oh. Thank you. (*He thinks for a moment then retrieves the publicity still. He inscribes it and hands it to ELSA.*) Here.

ELSA: (*Reading it.*) Oh, that's eh, that's…

RAVENCLIFFE: Is it alright or –

ELSA: Yeah, yeah it's, it's incredibly sweet. Thank you. Really, thank you. (*A brief moment. Finally ELSA gestures towards her phone to get back on track.*) So, Peter De Courcy…

RAVENCLIFFE: Oh yes. Peter rang me with an offer. He'd landed himself a directing gig on *Hammer House of Horror*, the TV spin-off, and he wanted me to read for it. But not a carriage driver this time, a lead. And after about 300 rounds of auditions the TV heads finally relented and let Peter have his way.

ELSA: And the episode was –

RAVENCLIFFE: 'Children of Selene'.

ELSA: Never been a huge werewolf fan myself. Bar *American Werewolf in London* obviously.

RAVENCLIFFE: Despite its lycanthropic excesses, 'Children of Selene' was really rather good. Peter had a real vision and he elevated the material into something almost, well, lyrical. That little episode of television helped launch him. And re-launched me too.

ELSA: (*Beat.*) You've said in the past that if you hadn't been cast by De Courcy you would have faded into obscurity. Do you really believe that?

RAVENCLIFFE: Yes, I do. There was no reason to think that was going to change if I'd stayed in Rep. That TV episode was the calling card I needed –

ELSA: And you went to Hollywood. Straight after?

RAVENCLIFFE: Two days after it aired. I knew this was my last chance so I was determined to make the most of it. Although some would argue that a decade of failed pilots and infomercials about food blenders hardly constitutes making the most of anything. It was useful for contacts though –

ELSA: Yeah, coz it was around this time you met Roger Corman. 1994?

RAVENCLIFFE: Yes. I bumped into Roger at parties and we'd talk. I loved his Poe adaptations and was quick to tell him.

ELSA: Flattery will get you everywhere.

RAVENCLIFFE: It certainly did with Corman. I did like him though. He was different to most people in Hollywood. Don't get me wrong, I wouldn't trust him as far as I could throw him, but at least he had something interesting to say. So when he mentioned he was setting up Concorde in Galway I asked him to keep me in mind and in fairness to him he did.

ELSA: I see.

RAVENCLIFFE: I arrived in Dublin on a Saturday and I was on set in Galway on Monday morning. Playing the creepy scientist in *Carnosaur 2*. Never to be confused with the infinitely inferior *Carnosaur 3*.

ELSA: (*Smiling.*) Right.

RAVENCLIFFE: All the stories about Concorde are true by the way. You heard about the cars?

ELSA: No.

RAVENCLIFFE: Most of the films made there were set in America, for commercial reasons. So Corman would import American cars and spray paint them different colors on either side. Then drive them past the camera in opposite directions to make the street look busier.

ELSA: Seriously?

RAVENCLIFFE: Oh yes. Ingenious, when you think about it.

ELSA: Were you surprised when Andy Muschietti, the director of *It*, namechecked *Carnosaur 2* in *Empire* magazine recently?

RAVENCLIFFE: Namechecked it? He practically penned a love letter to its influence on his career.

ELSA: Were you surprised?

RAVENCLIFFE: Yes, I was surprised. Don't get me wrong, it was a wonderful little pick-me-up for my career. Apparently people have been going crazy trying to track it down online. I've been invited to several of those, what do you call them, eh, large group of fans queue up to pay for autographs –

ELSA: Conventions.

RAVENCLIFFE: That's it, conventions. And there's talk of a Blu-ray getting released.

ELSA: Would you do a commentary?

RAVENCLIFFE: I think I probably would.

ELSA: Well, I look forward to that. (*Beat*.) If it's okay, I'm going to come back to Concorde in a moment.

RAVENCLIFFE: Really? I have oodles more Corman stories. I appeared in eleven of his movies by the time he'd had his fill of me. *Shadow of a Scream*, *Knocking on Death's Door*, *Knocking on Death's Door 2* –

ELSA: I'd like to spin back to your time with Peter De Courcy.

RAVENCLIFFE: (*Beat*.) You might have been better off conducting this interview with Pete considering how many questions you have about him.

ELSA: Might be a bit tricky considering he's been missing for the last three years. I don't suppose you know where he is, do you?

RAVENCLIFFE: No. Nobody does. (B*eat*.) Look, I think it's important to say that, despite Peter's... troubles he's never been anything less than a gentleman. At least in my presence. I don't know if that counts for anything in this day and age but, well... I always thought he was a grossly underrated director. All his talent was on show in 'Children of Selene'. Wonderfully visual storyteller, wicked sense of humour, the use of lighting –

ELSA: The scenes with a fourteen-year-old girl in her knickers?

RAVENCLIFFE: (*Smiling ruefully.*) Ah, I see. (*Beat as RAVENCLIFFE takes her in. He then rings a bell. After a moment MRS NEWMAN enters.*) Mrs Newman, could you clear away please? (*MRS NEWMAN does so. She goes to refill ELSA's glass.*)

ELSA: I'm finished, thank you.

MRS NEWMAN finishes clearing away the table and then leaves.

RAVENCLIFFE: I'm sorry, I'm really not comfortable talking about that after all this time.

ELSA: You must have known it was going to come up?

RAVENCLIFFE: I didn't think it was going to be today. (*ELSA holds his gaze. She isn't going to let this go.*) We were told that girl was seventeen. I saw the brief that was sent out by the production company. She lied, pure and simple. That or her agent bloody well did.

ELSA: You said we.

RAVENCLIFFE: (*Getting up to pour himself a large refill.*) What's that?

ELSA: You said *we* were told the girl was seventeen. Why would you have been told?

RAVENCLIFFE: I'd read the script and I was worried about the nature of that scene. I had some serious concerns, which proved to be justified.

ELSA: That's putting it mildly. Probably symptomatic of a different time –

RAVENCLIFFE: It was the 1980s, sweetheart, not the Middle Ages. Some of us knew the sight of a teenage Patsy Kensit lookalike prancing around in her smalls before turning into a fucking werewolf had the potential for trouble. I pleaded with Peter to double-check, no triple-check the girl's birth cert, and he assured me they already had. No one, and I mean no one was more disgusted by all this when it came out than me.

ELSA: (*Beat.*) There were all kinds of rumours about that shoot, wild parties that got out of hand –

RAVENCLIFFE: No different to any shoot back then.

ELSA: Stories about orgies –

RAVENCLIFFE: None of which involved that girl. I can say that categorically.

ELSA: So there were orgies –

RAVENCLIFFE: Now you're just putting words in my mouth –

ELSA: How can you categorically say the girl wasn't involved in something that didn't take place?

RAVENCLIFFE: I thought this was supposed to be a serious interview, not some sort of tabloid –

ELSA: I'm just trying to get the full picture of what went on –

RAVENCLIFFE: The full picture? Really?

ELSA: Yes. I think it's important to my readers –

RAVENCLIFFE: Diana Dors. Me. On numerous occasions. I mean, is that the kind of thing that you want to hear?

ELSA: What's Diana Dors got to do with this?

RAVENCLIFFE: She was in 'Children of Selene.'

ELSA: I know. She played the old lady.

RAVENCLIFFE: A lot of that was make-up. (*Smugly*.) Britain's Marilyn Monroe.

ELSA: Well, you didn't get her at her absolute best now, did you?

RAVENCLIFFE: I beg your pardon?

ELSA: Normally it's the creepy older actor groping the young starlet –

RAVENCLIFFE: What did you say?

ELSA: You know exactly what I mean.

RAVENCLIFFE: Show some respect.

ELSA: Respect? What are you going on about?

RAVENCLIFFE: (*Angrily*.) I said show some respect.

ELSA: (*Forceful*.) Don't shout at me.

RAVENCLIFFE: I wasn't shouting, believe me.

ELSA: Whatever it was, please don't do it again.

RAVENCLIFFE: Or what?

ELSA: I'm sorry?

RAVENCLIFFE: If I 'shout' at you again, what are you going to do? (*He stands.*) Well?

ELSA: (*She stands.*) I'm sorry, I don't feel very comfortable –

RAVENCLIFFE: (*Moving towards her.*) Wait. There's a few things I want to get cleared up.

ELSA: Excuse me please? (*She gathers her things.*)

RAVENCLIFFE: Hold on. Can we not discuss this?

ELSA: Excuse me.

RAVENCLIFFE: (*Sharply.*) Just hold on. This interview isn't over. (*ELSA hurries to leave but distracted by RAVENCLIFFE she trips and bangs her head on the table as she falls. She groans, tries to get up but can't. She lies back on the floor. RAVENCLIFFE watches her with rising panic.*) Elsa? Are you…? (*ELSA groans again but then stops. RAVENCLIFFE watches her. He doesn't move. After a moment…*) Mrs Newman? Mrs Newman?!

The lights dim. MRS NEWMAN enters and examines ELSA, checks her pulse. She beckons to RAVENCLIFFE to help her. Together they get ELSA back into her chair. MRS NEWMAN sees ELSA's phone on the table and pockets it. As this happens we hear a female voice. (NB: not ELSA's voice.)

FEMALE VO: Hello? HELLO?! Can anybody hear me? Listen, this isn't funny anymore. (*A faint sound of chanting.*) Hey! Whatever you think was happening here is… (*The chanting grows louder.*) You. Wait. What are you doing? You can't… get off me. (*She starts screaming.*) GET OFF ME!!!!

Lights slowly fade.

SCENE 2

Sometime later. RAVENCLIFFE stands beside the fireplace watching ELSA who is still out cold. MRS NEWMAN hovers by the door.

RAVENCLIFFE: How much longer do you think she'll be out for?

NEWMAN: I have absolutely no idea.

RAVENCLIFFE: Is she alright?

NEWMAN: Yes I think so.

RAVENCLIFFE: You think so?

NEWMAN: Yes.

RAVENCLIFFE: But are you sure?

NEWMAN: Do you see any certificates on the walls that would lead you to believe that I studied medicine?

RAVENCLIFFE: No.

NEWMAN: Then with respect can you stop asking me fucking questions about whether or not the girl that you hit is going to be alright?

RAVENCLIFFE: I didn't hit her, it was an accident. She fell over.

NEWMAN: So you told me.

MRS NEWMAN looks at him. He realises he hasn't fully convinced her.

RAVENCLIFFE: She kept pestering me, badgering me, questioning me about –

NEWMAN: Questioning you about what?

RAVENCLIFFE: 'Children of Selene'. Diana Dors.

NEWMAN: (*Grimacing.*) Oh.

RAVENCLIFFE: And Peter De Courcy.

NEWMAN: What did you say?

RAVENCLIFFE: Nothing. There's nothing to say. (*Beat. He gestures towards ELSA.*) This is serious, Mrs Newman.

NEWMAN: Oh I know.

RAVENCLIFFE: The door. (*He hands MRS NEWMAN a key which she reluctantly takes and then goes and locks the door.*) I don't suppose you have smelling salts back there by any chance?

NEWMAN: Why on earth would I have smelling salts back there?

RAVENCLIFFE: I don't know, I just thought –

NEWMAN: What do you think I do in there? Well?

RAVENCLIFFE: I have no idea.

NEWMAN: Exactly. (*ELSA starts to stir so they switch their attention back to her.*) Can we concentrate on this for now?

RAVENCLIFFE: Fine. (*ELSA stirs.*)

ELSA: (*Still groggy.*) Jesus, my head – (S*he moves her hands up to her head. Sees RAVENCLIFFE.*) You stay away from me.

RAVENCLIFFE: Miss Crenshaw. I am truly sorry about what happened. You have to believe me when I say it was an unfortunate –

ELSA makes for the door. It's locked.

ELSA: What's going on here? Why is this door locked?

RAVENCLIFFE: We just want to have a conversation.

ELSA: You're going to be having a long one with my solicitor.

RAVENCLIFFE: Please. We just want to talk.

ELSA: What about?

RAVENCLIFFE: You've been asking a lot of questions about me, Miss Crenshaw.

ELSA: It is my job.

RAVENCLIFFE: Really? You get paid for this, do you?

ELSA: Sometimes.

RAVENCLIFFE: Sometimes?

ELSA: Sometimes in cash and sometimes in kind.

RAVENCLIFFE: I see.

ELSA: Why is this important?

RAVENCLIFFE: Just trying to get a picture of your financial situation.

ELSA: My financial situation is just fine, thank you.

RAVENCLIFFE: Oh, we both know that that's a lie.

ELSA: Again, why is this important and why aren't we talking about me being locked in a fucking room? (*To MRS NEWMAN.*) What are you looking at, Nurse Ratched?

RAVENCLIFFE: (*To ELSA.*) You would do well to mind your manners.

ELSA: You're right, of course. My manners are what's truly important right now. Not being forcibly held against my will.

RAVENCLIFFE: You seem to be focusing on two projects from my past. 'Children of Selene' and *Carnosaur 2*. Why those?

ELSA: I happen to really like 'Selene' and *Carnosaur 2* is currently red hot. Despite its utter, irredeemable awfulness.

RAVENCLIFFE: Insulting your interviewee. That's an interesting tactic. Did they teach you that in blogging school?

ELSA: It's called *Carnosaur 2*, for fuck sake. We're not talking about high art here.

RAVENCLIFFE: You see, while I understand your interest in 'Selene', given the myths that have grown around it, *Carnosaur 2* couldn't have been any more different. Painless shoot, no on-set drama, a straight-to-video release that would have never have seen the light of day again except for some hip director falling in love with it.

ELSA: At least you're honest.

RAVENCLIFFE: So what's your angle here?

ELSA: Angle?

RAVENCLIFFE: For blackmail, presumably.

ELSA: (*Sniggering.*) For what, sorry?

RAVENCLIFFE: Blackmail.

ELSA: You? Why on earth –

RAVENCLIFFE: Come on, you've heard the rumours.

ELSA: About?

RAVENCLIFFE: *It: Chapter Two.*

ELSA: What's *It: Chapter Two* got to do with you?

RAVENCLIFFE: Such a pity this went the way it did. I would have given you a nice exclusive. Oh well.

ELSA: You've been cast? What part?

RAVENCLIFFE: That I'm not at liberty to say.

ELSA: Mhmm.

RAVENCLIFFE: Mhmm what?

ELSA: It's just, well, bringing back Travolta and Pam Grier from the dead is one thing but Jonathan Ravencliffe? Seems a bit of a stretch.

RAVENCLIFFE: Muschietti just made Warner Brothers 600 million on a 35-million-dollar budget. He can cast George fucking Lazenby if he wants. Given I'm about to come into something of a windfall and the kind of information you've been searching for, it suggests that you are after something. So what is it you want?

ELSA: How do you know what kinds of information I've been searching for?

RAVENCLIFFE: What do you think, I just shut myself off from the world, living out here in the middle of nowhere, oblivious to what's going on?

ELSA: Pretty much, yeah.

RAVENCLIFFE: Unfortunately for you, that is absolutely not the case. Certain activities or questions about certain people or incidents from my past elicit… interest.

ELSA: What, you monitor people? (*Gesturing towards MRS NEWMAN.*) You and her? Did you do an online seniors' course together?

RAVENCLIFFE: Very droll. For the final time – what's your angle here? (*Pause as ELSA realises she may have bitten off more than she can chew.*) It's about money, isn't it?

ELSA: No.

RAVENCLIFFE: Really?

ELSA: And I genuinely do like 'Children of Selene.'

NEWMAN: Seriously? (*RAVENCLIFFE seems both surprised and annoyed.*) Sorry, it's just never been a favourite of mine.

RAVENCLIFFE: I…

ELSA: But *Carnosaur 2*, well… do you remember the second AD?

RAVENCLIFFE: Of course I don't. Why would I?

ELSA: Yeah, why would you? Second ADs, ten a penny right?

RAVENCLIFFE: They certainly were when Corman was concerned.

ELSA: I'd probably be able to jog your memory better if I had some nude pictures of her, but alas…

RAVENCLIFFE: I beg your pardon, what did you just say?

ELSA: I'm sure there'd be a birthmark or an identifying feature that would spark something in you, but I never came across one of those. When I was going through my mother's things.

RAVENCLIFFE: (*Beat.*) Ah.

ELSA: Yeah.

RAVENCLIFFE: What age did you say you were?

ELSA: I didn't.

RAVENCLIFFE: And I'm supposed to be your father, is that it?

ELSA: According to my Mum.

NEWMAN: Nonsense.

RAVENCLIFFE: Exactly.

ELSA: You're so sure? Absolutely no chance –

RAVENCLIFFE: Absolutely no chance.

ELSA: That's not how she portrayed it.

NEWMAN: What a surprise.

ELSA: Sorry?

NEWMAN: You think you're the first twenty- or thirty-something to come knocking on his door, claiming all sorts of rubbish?

ELSA: I honestly don't –

NEWMAN: Let me guess, he promised your mother it was the real thing, that it was more than a film set romance, that she was the one? Well, am I warm?

ELSA: Yes. Among other things –

NEWMAN: I remember her.

ELSA: You do?

NEWMAN: Oh yes. Who do think cleans up his mess? Very pretty. Very young. Very fucking annoying. (*To RAVENCLIFFE.*) You honestly don't remember her?

RAVENCLIFFE: No. Should I?

NEWMAN: Corman had to fire her.

RAVENCLIFFE: Corman fired everyone.

NEWMAN: Even by your standards, she was a nightmare. Bawling her eyes out, causing scenes, saying she was going to kill herself when you'd finished with her.

RAVENCLIFFE: Oh her. Jesus.

ELSA: She tried to. Kill herself, I mean.

NEWMAN: I suppose she failed at that too?

ELSA: Don't you dare speak about my mother like that. (*To RAVENCLIFFE.*) You wanted to know what my angle was? I wanted you to acknowledge her, to acknowledge that she made an impression on you. That she existed in the same orbit as you, even briefly. Instead she's a fucking… benchmark for all the crazy bitches you've had to dump after you've had your way with them.

RAVENCLIFFE: Have you finished? First of all, your mother was a grown woman.

ELSA: She was twenty-two.

RAVENCLIFFE: And secondly, this was in the 1990s, not the eighteenth century. She was hardly cast out into the wilds of Connemara with a scarlet letter sewn into her dress.

ELSA: Twenty-two and pregnant by a man who wanted nothing to do with her –

RAVENCLIFFE: I offered to –

ELSA: Oh, I can imagine exactly what you offered to do. Pay for her to get the boat across to England, was it? Or did you go mad and get her a plane ticket? What a perfect gentleman. Have you any idea what a cliché you are? Seriously?

RAVENCLIFFE: (*Moving towards her.*) Don't you dare speak to me like that. (*RAVENCLIFFE has become very angry. It looks genuinely dangerous for ELSA.*)

NEWMAN: Don't rise to it, Jonathan.

RAVENCLIFFE: I think we might be past that point. (*A moment where this thought hangs in the air. They gather themselves, unsure how to proceed. RAVENCLIFFE studies ELSA.*) You don't look anything like her.

ELSA: I must take after you.

RAVENCLIFFE: You don't look anything like me either. (*He studies her again, more closely this time.*) Is she really your mother?

ELSA: Yes.

RAVENCLIFFE: Stop playing games. Is she your mother?

ELSA: (*After a long pause.*) No.

RAVENCLIFFE: Ah.

ELSA: I met her though. The second AD. She had some very interesting things to say about you.

RAVENCLIFFE: I'll bet. Why are you really here?

ELSA: (*Ignoring him, to MRS NEWMAN.*) How long have you worked for him?

NEWMAN: Since 1989.

ELSA: Then you know where most of the bodies are buried?

NEWMAN: There aren't any bodies, Miss Crenshaw.

ELSA: You've only worked for him since '89 but presumably you know all the stories about 'Children of Selene'?

NEWMAN: I've heard them but I've always treated them with the disdain they deserve.

RAVENCLIFFE: They're urban myths.

ELSA: When Peter De Courcy was –

NEWMAN: I've never met Peter De Courcy.

ELSA: But you knew about –

NEWMAN: Of course I did. It was an open secret the kind of vile creature he was. I told Mr Ravencliffe I would leave my job immediately if he had anything further to do with him.

ELSA: (*To RAVENCLIFFE*) When the allegations started against De Courcy, his victims came forth in their droves.

RAVENCLIFFE: And?

ELSA: One person was noticeable by her absence however.

RAVENCLIFFE: Who?

ELSA: The girl from 'Children of Selene.'

RAVENCLIFFE: Your point being?

ELSA: That never struck you as odd? I mean it was the first real example of De Courcy's –

RAVENCLIFFE: No, it never struck me as odd.

ELSA: I've been able to track down pretty much everyone that worked on that TV show. Everyone except her. And De Courcy, of course.

RAVENCLIFFE: It was made in 1980. God knows what could have happened to that girl in the subsequent years.

ELSA: Or what could have happened to her at the time.

RAVENCLIFFE: Really? This fairy tale again?

ELSA: I think it's true.

RAVENCLIFFE: (*Laughing.*) Jesus. What was it? She was murdered in a satanic ritual? Or was it just a mundane, dirty little sex game that went terribly wrong? I get them mixed up. It's easy given how many versions of this story there are.

ELSA: De Courcy hinted at something way bigger than just him.

RAVENCLIFFE: Yes, in order to throw people off the scent –

ELSA: I think it's true and I think the footage exists.

RAVENCLIFFE: This is ridiculous –

ELSA: I think you have it and I think it's here.

NEWMAN: Why would Jonathan have it? And if he did, why would he hang on to it?

RAVENCLIFFE: Exactly.

ELSA: Leverage.

RAVENCLIFFE: Against whom?

ELSA: De Courcy. You make an innocent mistake on set. The girl and her agent said she was seventeen and they triple-checked her birth cert. You make a mistake, De Courcy holds it over you and you discover something about De Courcy beyond your wildest, sickest dreams. (*RAVENCLIFFE is trying not to give anything away but there is a momentary flicker.*) I mean, I could be wrong but –

RAVENCLIFFE: (*Shaking his head.*) Such a coincidence that this happens just as I'm about to make my comeback.

ELSA: This story is happening, Jonathan. It's up to you to decide what part you play in it.

RAVENCLIFFE: How much do you want?

ELSA: No one even knows her real name. The girl's. Were you aware of that? Hmm? (*No reaction from RAVENCLIFFE.*) I didn't think so. The one she's listed as in the credits is wrong. She never did anything beforehand and we know she never did anything afterwards. She was from the north, we can tell that from her accent. How did she end up in London? Was she a runaway? Was she in love and followed her heart? Was she talent-spotted and given someone's card? It's like she never truly existed, like she only ever existed in stories told in certain circles. Well, I think she deserves better than that. I think she's more than an urban myth, more than a, what did you call it? A fairy tale. And she's probably one of God knows how many others. So if De Courcy was responsible for her death and if you knew about it and did nothing, then there will be a reckoning.

RAVENCLIFFE: Not to mention a worldwide exclusive for your little blog. (*He lets that one sit for a moment.*) And you're the one to deliver it, are you? This reckoning?

ELSA: Somebody has to.

RAVENCLIFFE: And how do you propose to do that, locked in this room?

ELSA: It's not too late. For you. To do the right thing. You know that's what you have to do, deep inside. How long have you lived with this –

RAVENCLIFFE: I haven't lived with anything.

ELSA: This is your last chance, Jonathan. You have to see that. Things like this can only stay hidden for so long. You made a mistake, pure and simple. You slept with a… barely underage girl. You weren't to know –

RAVENCLIFFE: I didn't sleep with that girl –

ELSA: You don't deserve to be lumped into the same category as perverts like De Courcy –

RAVENCLIFFE: Be quiet –

ELSA: You're not some sort of sick –

RAVENCLIFFE: Shut up.

ELSA: – bastard that'll be stuck in solitary confinement for his own protection. A nonce that has his walls covered in shit and piss whenever there's a –

RAVENCLIFFE: Stop.

ELSA: – that has his teeth knocked out to stop him from biting whenever he's about to –

RAVENCLIFFE: That's not me.

ELSA: But that's what people are going to think you are unless you get out in front of it. (*This registers with RAVENCLIFFE.*) Jonathan –

RAVENCLIFFE: That's rubbish.

ELSA: You know I'm right.

NEWMAN: Jonathan.

RAVENCLIFFE: (*Wavering.*) I didn't, I wasn't… I would never have –

NEWMAN: You would never have what?

RAVENCLIFFE: I was there but I didn't –

ELSA: But you didn't what?

RAVENCLIFFE: I didn't –

NEWMAN: Jonathan?

RAVENCLIFFE: I was there, but I didn't kill her. (*To MRS NEWMAN.*) Please, Gloria, you have to believe me. (*MRS NEWMAN moves away from him.*) It was a terrible mistake that…

ELSA: De Courcy? What did he –

RAVENCLIFFE: Caught me. Caught us. In bed. Told me the girl's real age. Threatened to go to the papers, said he'd destroy my career. Tried to recruit me into his horrible little cabal. Said he recognised a kindred spirit. I never was, I swear. I just went along with it to try and get something back on him, leverage like you said, and that's when I saw, that's when he, with the girl, he… I never knew people were capable of such…

ELSA: How did she die?

RAVENCLIFFE: A knife. Some sort of ceremony that got out of hand –

NEWMAN: Why didn't you go to the police?

RAVENCLIFFE: I… I panicked. I thought I was implicated. I was there, I didn't stop it, I couldn't stop it and that meant that…

NEWMAN: You lied to me. You lied to my face… (*RAVENCLIFFE goes towards her.*) Do not come near me. (*RAVENCLIFFE stops.*) I've worked for you for nearly 30 years. I've, I've done everything for you. I've booked every flight, negotiated every contract, paid off every bill. I've waited outside every audition, every dressing room, every trailer. I accompanied you on every hospital visit. I helped you choose this house, went to auctions with you to pick out the furniture –

RAVENCLIFFE: Mrs Newman –

NEWMAN: When you couldn't get a job for six years, I stayed with you. Stayed loyal to you. Why? Because I believed in you, cared about you, cared about your career. Our career. And this was all built on a lie? Worse, built on a –

RAVENCLIFFE: No, no, it's –

NEWMAN: Every memory I have of you is rotten. Everything we've ever shared is decaying right in front of my eyes. I can't, I just – (*MRS NEWMAN has to sit down.*)

ELSA: (*Beat.*) Where's the footage? Of the girl's murder?

RAVENCLIFFE: There isn't any –

ELSA: Give up the act. Where –

RAVENCLIFFE: I told you –

ELSA: Is it in there, in that locked drawer? Hmm? (*She gestures to RAVENCLIFFE's desk.*) You like to keep mementoes close by.

RAVENCLIFFE: What did you say?

ELSA: You heard me.

RAVENCLIFFE: Did I not just –

ELSA: Go and get us the key then.

RAVENCLIFFE: (*To ELSA.*) How did you know where the footage was?

ELSA: (*Ruefully.*) Jonathan… (*RAVENCLIFFE realises he's hung himself.*)

RAVENCLIFFE: You – (*RAVENCLIFFE moves to the drawer. He fumbles with the key and then gets it open. He starts to rummage, desperate to find the footage. MRS NEWMAN moves closer to ELSA. His face contorts into a fit of rage as he realises the footage isn't there.*) Where the fuck is it? (*He starts towards ELSA. As he's about to reach her, MRS NEWMAN stands in front of ELSA, protecting her.*)

NEWMAN: Jonathan. Enough.

She holds his gaze until the fight starts to leave him. MRS NEWMAN and ELSA walk backwards towards the door. MRS NEWMAN hands the key to

ELSA who unlocks it. They exit and then lock it, keeping RAVENCLIFFE inside. He paces for a moment, refills his wine glass, slumps into his chair and stares into the abyss. Outside MRS NEWMAN takes out ELSA's phone and hands it to her.

NEWMAN: I left it recording.

ELSA takes the phone and stops it recording. Beat. ELSA gathers herself.

ELSA: It was you, wasn't it? That sent the tip off about the footage?

NEWMAN: Yes.

ELSA: Why all the subterfuge?

NEWMAN: I wanted to hear it from him. I wanted him to admit it. To eh, what is it you say these days? To own it.

ELSA: Yeah, own it. Still that was impressive. If I didn't know any better, I would have thought you were the actor.

NEWMAN: I did dabble a bit in my youth.

ELSA: You missed your calling, that was some academy award-winning – (*ELSA notices MRS NEWMAN looks a bit unsteady on her feet.*) Are you alright?

NEWMAN: A little bit shook.

ELSA: Understandable. I'm not feeling great myself. (B*eat. ELSA gets business-like.*) Where is it? The footage? Please don't tell me it's back in there? (*MRS NEWMAN reaches into her pocket and using a handkerchief pulls out a USB stick.*) Have you watched it?

NEWMAN: Yes. Well, some of it, I couldn't finish it.

ELSA: Oh. (*ELSA pockets the USB stick.*)

NEWMAN: So what now?

ELSA: I'm, I'm not exactly sure to be honest. I have a contact in the press, I'll get her advice. Maybe talk to a solicitor. Get this (*indicating her phone*) to the police.

NEWMAN: Good. Good.

ELSA: (*Beat.*) It's an incredibly brave thing that you've done.

NEWMAN: It doesn't feel very brave.

ELSA: It is.

NEWMAN: I'm just sorry I didn't find out sooner.

ELSA: That's not your fault.

NEWMAN: I know. I know it isn't, but still… Are you a fan of M. R. James, Elsa?

ELSA: I am. Why do you ask?

NEWMAN: If you're a fan of M. R. James, then you'll know that there's usually a terrible price to pay for digging up the past. Usually for the person doing the digging.

ELSA: Not this time, Mrs Newman. Not this time. (*ELSA places a hand on MRS NEWMAN's shoulder. MRS NEWMAN nods. ELSA breaks and starts to gather her things.*) All right then. I best get going. Thank you, Mrs Newman. For trusting me with this.

NEWMAN: I'm glad it was someone like you. (*ELSA smiles at her and then starts to exit.*) Elsa. Will you write about it?

ELSA: I'm not sure yet. Probably. When the time is right. If you're okay with it –

NEWMAN: You should. You should write about it. All of it.

ELSA nods then exits. MRS NEWMAN stares after her, then looks back at the house. Lights slowly fade.

THE END

Also Available:

Freshly Brewed (2008)

Twelve short plays from Bewley's Café Theatre

Edited by Declan Meade and Emily Firetog
with an introduction by Christopher Fitz-Simon
and a foreword by Mark O'Halloran

The Plays:

Too Much of Nothing by Mark O'Halloran & David Wilmot

Bad Sunday by Mark Wale

The Head of Red O'Brien by Mark O'Halloran

The Star Trap by Michael James Ford

Fred and Jane by Sebastian Barry

One Too Many Mornings by Mark O'Halloran & David Wilmot

Election Night by Donal Courtney

So Long, Sleeping Beauty by Isobel Mahon

Jimmy Joyced! by Donal O'Kelly

Buridan's Ass by S. R. Plant

Two for a Girl by Mary Kelly & Noni Stapleton

Is There Balm in Gilead? by Michael Harding

"This book of short plays produced at Bewley's Café Theatre, could be said to be a celebration of not just one, but two miracles in Dublin cultural life – the always interesting, innovative and well-used small space that is Bewley's Café Theatre and the continued strength of Declan Meade's Stinging Fly Press, which adds this impressive volume to a steadily growing list of excellent publications."

Dermot Bolger, *The Sunday Business Post*

ISBN: 978-1906539-04-7 | €18.00

stingingfly.org

The Stinging Fly magazine was established in late 1997 to seek out, publish and promote the very best new Irish and international writing. We published our first issue in March 1998. We have a particular interest in encouraging new writers, and in promoting the short story form. We now publish two issues of *The Stinging Fly* each year: in May and November. It is available on subscription from our website. Subscribers receive free access to our complete archive of back issues.

The Stinging Fly Press was launched in May 2005 with the publication of our first title, *Watermark* by Sean O'Reilly. The Press continues to work in tandem with the magazine and shares its interest in discovering new writers and promoting short stories.

Our other titles include:

There Are Little Kingdoms by Kevin Barry (2007)
Life in The Universe by Michael J. Farrell (2009)
Young Skins by Colin Barrett (2013)
Pond by Claire-Louise Bennett (2015)
Dinosaurs On Other Planets by Danielle McLaughlin (2015)
The Springs of Affection by Maeve Brennan (2016)
The Long-Winded Lady by Maeve Brennan (2017)
Levitation by Sean O'Reilly (2017)
Sweet Home by Wendy Erskine (2018)
Show Them A Good Time by Nicole Flattery (2019)

visit www.stingingfly.org

Thank you for supporting independent publishing.